ONE GAME AT A TIME

WHY SPORTS MATTER

MATT HERN

AK PRESS
EDINBURGH • OAKLAND • BALTIMORE

One Game at a Time: Why Sports Matter
By Matt Hern

© 2013 Matt Hern
This edition © 2013 AK Press (Oakland, Edinburgh, Baltimore)
ISBN: 978-1-84935-136-2
e-ISBN: 978-1-84935-137-9
Library of Congress Control Number: 2013930245

AK Press	AK Press UK
674-A 23rd Street	PO Box 12766
Oakland, CA 94612	Edinburgh EH8 9YE
USA	Scotland
www.akpress.org	www.akuk.com
akpress@akpress.org	ak@akedin.demon.co.uk

The above addresses would be delighted to provide you with the latest AK Press distribution catalog, which features several thousand books, pamphlets, zines, audio and video recordings, and gear, all published or distributed by AK Press. Alternately, visit our websites to browse the catalog and find out the latest news from the world of anarchist publishing:
www.akpress.org | www.akuk.com
revolutionbythebook.akpress.org

Printed in the United States on recycled, acid-free paper.

Cover by CDS
Interior by Margaret Killjoy | birdsbeforethestorm.net

CONTENTS

ACKNOWLEDGMENTS

A lot of people are going to be relieved I finally got this book written. I have been cornering friends and family (and lots people who don't fit into either category) and hitting them with this stuff for a long time now. I've test-run, reconsidered, and revised this argument over many years: sometimes lucidly, sometimes less so, sometimes soberly, sometimes drunkenly, sometimes passionately, sometimes irrationally, and often at tiresome length. So to all of you who have endured and engaged me, thanks so much for your tolerance and generosity.

Parts of this book were published in *The Tyee*, *Vancouver Magazine*, *Left Hook Journal*, and *Z Magazine*, so thanks to all for allowing me more formal chances to get valuable feedback.

More specifically though a number of people have given me really useful and smart input on this text: Geoff Mann, Richard Lawley, Jillian Dheri, Riley Hern, Kelsey Blair, Selena Couture, Dan Grego, Isaac Oommen, Chuck Morse, and Sarah Kendall all provided terrific critiques and responses. You guys will hear some of yourselves in here I am sure.

None were more helpful, though, than the indomitable Kate Khatib, my editor at AK Press who was supportive and scathing in just the right doses and pushed this book into far better territory.

Much love and respect for the mighty Caffé Roma Sports Bar where much of this book was written.

My deepest gratitude, as always, is owed to my families: my island family, especially Adele, Gan and Sean, and to all my East Van family, most especially Selena, Sadie, and Daisy (and Diana, Ashley, Keith, et al.) for listening so often and so patiently, for sitting through endless recaps of games, watching inane internet clips, abiding my distractions, and nursing me through my (many) injuries. They have asked about the sports I love, cheered when I cheer, sympathized when I have been beaten, allowed me to bask in my victories, acknowledged my heartbreaks, and watched so many games with me. They have cared because I care, which is as loving as I could ever ask.

And of course, more than anyone, this book is for my father, Riley Hern. His inexhaustible love for tennis, the Canucks, and for sporting events of all kinds has been matched by his lifelong patience and kindness towards all children as they learned to play under his watch. He was in my head always as I wrote this and I can only hope that a little bit of his sweet and generous heart shines through.

CHAPTER 1:

GETTING OUR HEADS IN THE GAME

SPORTS AS A FIELD OF RADICAL POSSIBILITIES

I want to make an argument in favor of sports.

Playing sports for sure, but also watching, following, cheering, fanning, obsessing, dorking out, believing, caring, really caring. I want you to *care* about sports, whether or not you pay any attention to them or even have much interest. I want you to think about the sporting world as a legitimate site for struggle and politics—and not in that cutesy grad-school, high theory/low-culture, check-out-my-lowbrow-street-cred, critical-ethnology vein. I mean in the most everyday, obvious way as a legitimate site for struggle and politics.

It's essentially impossible to avoid sports. High-performance or quotidian, on TVs in bars or at home, in stadiums, parks, and schools, on t-shirts, in ads, gossip columns, and endless banter, sports are everywhere, and they're usually neon-flashing-and-hollering right up in our faces. And, of course, there is a full range of responses: lots of people eat that shit right up and identify proudly and profoundly with their local pro team; many people just love to play and build their lives around it; others resent and loathe sports in any guise; and many, maybe most, folks feel varying levels of ambivalence towards the formalized play that is sports and shifting degrees of simultaneous attraction and antipathy towards the overhyped, hyper-corporatized professional gong-show spectacles that cast their shadow over all our games.

It doesn't take much psychoanalytical posturing to understand that those adult relationships with sports are in large part governed by our experiences as kids. For many people, sports were irreplaceably vibrant parts of growing up—primary sources of pride, exuberance, and community. For others, sports were childhood sites of shame and exclusion, humiliation, and violence. Lots of us probably experienced variants of both situations, and for many, the experience was just OK, not particularly compelling one way or another, just something to be negotiated as painlessly as possible.

Across the globe, sports dominate many, perhaps even most, childhoods. So many kids find that their sense of self-worth, community standing, and possibility is tied to fraught intersections with the world of sports that run the full gamut from totally fucked to beautiful. Our adult experience and analyses naturally reflect (and construct) this ongoing relationship, which means that writing and talking about sports is always (if often obliquely and/or obtusely) talking about childhood.

Yet I want to shoot a simultaneously broad and specific challenge across this whole spectrum of experience, and our relationship to sports. If you love sports but can't see a legit connection to progressive or radical politics, I want to make a case here. If you hate sports and think they're barbaric, let me try to convince you—not why you should *like* them, but why you should respect the sports world. If you are tolerantly befuddled, bemused, ambivalent, or have a passable (dis)interest, I submit that the particular characteristics and contours of the sporting world open up radical possibilities that are not readily available elsewhere, and that should be embraced.

I am convinced that sports offers us an arena where we can resist neoliberal logics and bodily encounter liberatory ideals. The trick, however, is to take that (direct and/or vicarious) experience and tie it to larger social and political thinking, so that the specific kinds of trust, mutual aid, and generosity that abound in sports become not just isolated personal connections, but a force for the common good. I'm talking about sports specifically here, in part because that's what occupies most of my head, but really it's an argument about difference, or better put, neighborliness and friendship.

Capitalism has exacted conquest across every social and cultural sphere of our lives—maybe nowhere more so than sports—but this is not fate and the sporting world is worth fighting for, for specific reasons and more generalized political ones, too. Far too few of us (regardless of our existing relationships with sports) really take up that offer properly, but it's just sitting there. In a cynical and catastrophic era when so many possibilities seem so dim, that's a powerful project the Left has disdained for far too long. It's high time to take it up.

GIVING IT 110%

It's pretty common to condescend to sports as territory really only fit for hormone-addled teens, Neanderthals, and developmentally-delayed retrogrades. Sort of strangely, this attitude shows up in a whole variety of guises, constantly embedded, reiterated, and repercussed by sports fans, casual observers, and antagonists alike, and amounts to an assumptive abandonment of the sporting world as worthy of serious engagement.

Sophisticated "thinking" people of all ideological persuasions have seemingly always held condescending attitudes towards sports—and that's for lots of obvious reasons, and subtler ones that dovetail with a generalized disdain (from the left as much as the right) for working-class, everyday culture. Aside from the occasional Plimpton-esque (or Mailer/Oates/Remnick-esque) quasi-anthropological foray, intellectuals (and I'm using that term as loosely as imaginable) overwhelmingly dismiss the sporting world.

No less than Noam Chomsky articulated a cheap (but super common) line when he suggested that if people paid as much attention to politics as they do to sports we'd have a much better world.[1] It's the frequent default stance of leftists, progressives, and liberals everywhere, even those who love sports: this tired old position that sports are the contemporary opiate of the masses. But Noam never would have said that about music, dance, theater, painting, or poetry, and that contradiction is what I'm after here. I want us to consider sports as seriously as we take other "high" art forms, to understand sports as sitting squarely within a spectrum of creative expression, and just as worthy of our serious attention, engagement, reflection, love, and respect. Sports and art are *not* the same thing, but those delineations are arbitrary ones, and they largely exist to stabilize

---

1   Noam continued: "I suppose that's also one of the basic functions it [sports] serves in the society in general it occupies the population, and keeps them from trying to get involved with things that really matter." He said a lot more about sports here: http://terasima. gooside.com/article1sports2spectator.html

class pretensions and social positions. I suggest we eviscerate those definitions entirely. [2]

Chomsky's generalized position is echoed by all kinds of people—whether they spend much time thinking about sports or not—who tend to defer to this analytical refuge; it's an easy and clichéd place to wander off to. And to be sure, sports consistently give us every reason to revile them. Whether it's the a-hole football players from your high school, the idiot jock homophobe culture, the sexual assaults so endemic to athletics, the crazed militarism at pro events, or the fucking Washington Redskins, it ain't like sports aren't doing their honest best to drive good people away. In the face of all the mouth-breathing scorn jock culture heaps on others, it's hardly surprising that thoughtful people of every predilection aren't terribly impressed with the possibilities of the sports world, and refuse to return the respect that sports has denied them.

The presumption of the essential triviality of sports is visible (in a weirdly self-flagellating twitch) even among sports-nerds. Many of us are simultaneously obsessed and chagrined—as if sports aren't worthy of our legitimate attention. It's something we hide like the porn history on our computers, something that stains whatever fantasies we might have of being serious adults. Even on rabid sports talk radio, whenever a tragedy occurs commentators trot out an inevitably reflexive cliché: "Makes you think about what really matters…." As if sports *don't really matter*—when they clearly, absolutely do.

Across the ideological, class, cultural, and sporting spectrum, there seems to be a consensus that sports are, at best, distractingly vapid. This retreat by folks who love sports, and folks who revile them, and everyone in-between, has turned the sports world into easy prey for hyper-consumptive,

---

2   For a good discussion here, please see: Richard Schechner, *Performance Theory*, New York : Routledge, 1988.

violent, militaristic, sexist, and homophobic politics—and, ultimately, handed over the immense power of sports to some of the worst elements of our society. It's a retreat that has concretized a self-fulfilling prophecy and self-regulating narrative that tells us just how fucked sports really are. When the sporting world reinforces its own triviality, whether purposefully or not, it gives permission for its own consistently idiotic behavior, because, well, it just "doesn't matter" much. Hardly. My argument here is precisely the opposite: we should all—whether we watch, obsess, cheer, play, or not at all—take sports seriously, as worthy of real respect, because if we don't, we will continue to allow them to be dominated by some of the most regrettable politics imaginable.

Sports Illustrated estimates that 62% of American males and 47% of females regularly play competitive sports. Even more than playing, though, we like to watch: in the U.S., twenty-one of the forty-five most-watched TV shows in history are Super Bowls; in India, the most watched program of all time is the 2011 Cricket World Cup Final; in China, it is the opening ceremony of the 2008 Summer Olympic Games which (not coincidentally) remains the most watched global broadcast in history. In Germany, ten of the top eleven most watched broadcasts of all time are soccer games; in Canada, the most watched television broadcast in history is the men's gold-medal hockey game of 2010 Winter Olympics with 16.6 million viewers watching the entire game, roughly one-half of the country's population. These kinds of stats are repeated across the globe, whether we're talking TV or live events, numbers that will surprise approximately no one. Now, I don't want to equate television audiences with inherent value, but it sure as hell means *something*.

Big sporting events dominate cities, incite riots, and fill entire newspaper sections with relentless coverage of minutiae and gossip. Sports are the default topic of conversation at parties and bars the world over. Sports keep many families together, gives buddies something to talk about, and provide narrative shape for many of our days. Teams and players inspire devotion vastly beyond reason. There is something very deep here that even the ungodly amounts of garish marketing, ultra-nationalist tendencies, hyper-corporatism, and dislikable athletes with their tricked-out Hummers can't extinguish: so many of us love sports, both participating and spectating, for lots of very good and very valuable reasons.

I am obviously not defending the entire breadth of the sporting world as it exists now (!): what I am doing is arguing for what sports could be. To my mind it's not a great leap to think of a time when sports are a force for good in our culture and we condescend to those possibilities at our peril. That's what this book is after: I'm arguing that sports can, should, and do really matter.

RUNNING IT RIGHT UP THE GUT

That said, even for me, sometimes it seems totally fucking absurd to be making this argument. Sitting here watching a tepid mid-season Canucks game surrounded by a-holes in Affliction gear shouting grotesquely sexist/anti-queer shit at the ice while getting hammered on $8.50 plastic cups of Coors Light is hardly the place to feel comfortable about the transformative potential of sports.

Between periods I stroll around the concourse, dodging the Red Bull kiosks, the Pepsi girls, and the Stella stalls. I'm looking to milk a little extra value for the $127.50 mid-bowl tickets I've lucked into when a pal left town unexpectedly. It's a roiling river of people, and 87% of them are geared right up in team apparel.

Daunted, I duck into one of the metastasized merch stores inside the arena and scope out the $299 authentic jerseys, $45 pennants, $50 branded garden gnomes (!), $115 baseball hat display cases (!!), $79 ticket frames and the hundreds of other Canucks-themed ephemera.[3] I buy a pair of shot glasses for my mom's birthday. I'm not sure she's ever gunned a shot in her life, but it seems the right thing to do. I see a vintage Brendan Morrison signed and framed player card propped up by the counter so I snag that too. Mom's worth that for sure. She'll love it. The clerk wraps it for me expertly in Canucks-colored paper and slides it all into a lovely, tastefully-branded little Canucks-themed bag. Very nice.

Post-game, we slip into the sports bar at the corner, watch the highlights of the game we've just come from, and I then review the situation on espn.com before bed. There's scarcely been a moment over the last six hours when I haven't been a zombie-bug wandering in a manically-consumptive formicarium.

Most decent people instinctively act with revulsion in the face of this insane, corporatized, spectacular shit-show. And totally justifiably. The micro and macro-economic logics of the pro sports world are crazed and infuriating. Triple-figure tickets, billion-dollar franchises, $3 million Super Bowl ads, $13 million a year for middling pitchers, a quarter billion for A-Rod (twice!), stadium deals in the high hundreds of millions, that freaking $300 jersey, the commodification of players … there is almost nothing about the economics of the professional sporting world that makes any sense, or bears any rational relationship to the everyday lives of everyday people.

Capitalism has grotesquely distorted the sporting world, but what hasn't it maimed? What cultural quarter hasn't been reduced to corporate shilling? Think of dance centers named after banks, cigarette companies sponsoring operas, theater awards given out by mining companies, folk singers sponsored by Starbucks, and artists of every stripe controlled and traded as commodities. Professional sports have

---

3   Yup, these are real prices.

been wholly jacked by corporatist economics and neoliberal ideologies like everything else, just maybe a little more vibrantly and effusively—in part because sports are so powerful: where else are you going to find 100,000 people every Saturday afternoon?

Similarly, sports are often derided as offering another kind of economic opiate: holding out an impossible carrot to marginalized kids and communities that will ostensibly drag them out of poverty. And that's correct: really, only a tiny percentage of kids ever make it pro and 99.9% of us end up having to pursue some other ways to make rent. If we're talking about sports as a potential income generator, it's a real long shot (although no more so than music or acting or dancing), and there are certainly plenty of occupational hazards. But that's true of most any job, whether it's nursing, roofing, driving, doing construction, social working, farming, or firefighting. And many (most?) jobs have other kinds of hazards: physical, psychological, and/or emotional. Is it worse to get your melon dinged up and lose a few neurons than it is to sit in a dehumanizing, alienating, dignity-sapping workplace that costs you hope and imagination and vitality? There are costs and compromises to any occupation, professional or otherwise.

Regardless, I think it is very problematic (and maybe a little paternalistic) to critique sports as simply a poor career choice. People engage in creative pursuits, whether it's boxing, painting, basketball, singing, judo, dancing, or writing, not to get rich but because we love being creative: the act of individual and collaborative creativity is good in and of itself. A small subset of us get highly skilled at those pursuits, and then a much smaller subset still actively pursues a pro career in hoops, movies, the music business, fighting, or whatever. For most of my youth, I played ball seventeen hours a day and dreamed that I was Downtown Freddie Brown or Dennis Johnson, but was I planning for an NBA career? Well, I guess highly abstractly but not really. Ball wasn't a career move: it was pleasure, and it wasn't a failure or wasted effort when I fell far short.

I don't want to reduce creative expression to instrumentality and assess its value based on potential career earnings. Lives should not be managed like stock portfolios. The problem isn't that boxing or basketball or musical theater or hiphop or the trombone are not sure-fire routes out of economic marginalization. It's that long-shot lottery-winning dreams are necessary because, for so many folks, there is so little else to realistically hope for. To blame sports for not being able to fix the failures of capitalism is chasing the wrong squirrel up the wrong tree.

"FOOTBALL IS THE OPEN-AIR KINGDOM OF HUMAN LOYALTY"[4]

Not long ago I was speaking at the Baltimore Book Festival, giving a talk about ecological urbanism. It's a terrific and popular event, and our tent was full of people despite the fact that it was approximately 150 degrees outside and the tent smothered whatever little breeze might have been blowing. I was sitting on a panel, and when my turn came 'round, I did what I pretty much always do: I made a joke about sports.

It's a kind of a platitudinous speaker's cliché to drop an informal aside before launching into your shtick, but nevertheless I consistently do it, ostensibly to lighten things up a bit, to suggest to the audience that maybe I'm not a humorless twit, and maybe to relax me a little. I also tend to be talking to academic and/or activist audiences and I like to think it throws them off their game a bit. Maybe not so much, but you know.

I started this Baltimore talk by offhandedly chatting about the Ravens. I could feel the sweat rolling down my

---

4   A quote from Antonio Gramsci.

back like a faucet and I was towelling off every fifteen seconds. I had just come from a bar where I watched a wild Patriots-Bills game and was hoping to catch the Ravens later that afternoon, so it seemed like the right thing to do. Right away, an older African-American guy sitting in the front row scowled expansively and said loudly "Don't talk about sports!" I looked at him and said, "Why not? It was a great game." That wasn't the response he was hoping for apparently because he immediately stormed out.[5]

I didn't mind too much: I get people walking out on my talks here and there and figure that if you don't piss some people off you're being far too bland. I just carried on my way but as I was talking I could see the man at the back of the audience, listening in, but also waving his arms around and talking to people loudly and passionately. So I was prepared when the mic opened for questions and he barrelled in and proceeded to rip me a new one. He talked at some length about how disrespectful I was to be glib about something as meaningless as sports, that I was being wasteful of everyone's time when there were so many important issues to talk about and that talking about sports was just callow. He also mentioned that he really wanted to punch me "right in the face."

A fellow member of the panel was clearly freaked out and tried to diffuse the situation, and the audience visibly tensed up, but I kind of liked it. I mean I'm never thrilled about being so aggressively taken to task in public (or in private really!), but I was genuinely interested, even excited by his point, and took his threat as metaphorical, not actual.

---

5   It's probably worth noting that part of the reason he was upset was because the previous speakers had been discussing the foreclosure crisis and displacement in Baltimore as a result of a new biotech facility. That is some horrible shit that matters unequivocally and stirs up some deep feelings. I totally understand and support his pissed-offness.

I badly wanted to take the argument up, but it didn't seem like the right place to get into it, so I just said that I respected his opinion, was sorry that he was upset, but that I held to the value of sports and didn't think it was disrespectful in any way. Then we moved on.

Afterward I was talking with some members of the audience and I could see the guy waiting a row or two back, so I stuck out my hand and asked how he was doing. He was very gracious and apologized, complimented me on my talk, and said he appreciated my approach and analyses. I was friendly in return, thanked him for his apology, and offered my support and solidarity in the face of the outrageous bullshit his neighborhood is facing. It was clear though that we still had a difference of opinion that we didn't really address.

Baltimore is a majority-black city facing some very serious economic, social, and political challenges. The effects of deindustrialization, the mortgage crisis, suburban flight, crime, poverty, and corruption are readily evident at even half a glance. So it's highly understandable that a resident might get irritated with some random cocky white dude showing up and dropping blithe banter in the midst of some important and serious conversations. But in many ways this argument is exactly what I'm after: I'm convinced that sports really *are* worth talking about. Not just for their convivial, small-talky instrumentality. That's all good in itself, but sports can and should be part of those serious conversations too. Next time I'm in Baltimore, that's what I want to talk about for sure.

I also think watching and following sports is a worthy activity. It's common to suggest that *playing* sports is defensible but *spectating* is opiatical, passive, mind-numbing, and likely brain—if not soul—damaging.[6] I dispute this from

6   There's a layer here that I want to acknowledge, but not fully delve into because it heads off in a whole bunch of directions. It needs to

beginning to end. It would be crazy-talk to suggest that playing music is alright, but listening to it is a waste of time. Or that acting is good, but going to the theater is passive and consumptive. Or that you are creatively actualized if you make films, but somehow less-than if you watch them. We all know that music, movies, theater, dance, poetry, and all the rest are vibrant and legitimate sites of conversation and contestation for observers and critics as much as creators. Why not sports?

It is really important to understand sports comprehensively (and not as arbitrarily separate) as playing and watching; fanning and participating; pro, high performance, amateur, and everyday. There are obviously critical distinctions between each of those activities (and kinds of activities): they are not the same and carry all kinds of different weights, impacts, reverberations, and effects. But to understand sports we have to encounter them as a nexus of relationships that bind performers to text[7] to audience to critic to community.

---

be said that "spectating" is a broad category. Different types of spectating (in various places and through different media) have different ways of generating meaning and pleasure. Stopping by a neighborhood softball game, going to a huge stadium and watching sports spectacles on TV are very different activities. Sports are primarily spectated via television and thus viewers are engaged with and subjected to massive corporate-media-industry manipulations, with all the requisite complications. I am not suggesting that watching sports on TV is "bad" per se, but that spectating is a very broad category of activity that needs to be parsed. I will hit this more later.

7   I'm being a little cute and nodding at a certain thread here by using the word *text*. I'm suggesting that the specific constraints of specific sports allow for certain kinds of expressive relationships: I might have used the word *form*, but I think it is important to place this argument in the context of critical evaluations of texts. That's a performance theory nerd-note, but one that needs to be said.

The argument that names professional sports as *bad*, but playing in the park as *good*, is lazy and obscuring. We have to take it all on, and understand playing and watching, participating and spectating, performer and audience as bound up together, in part because observing skilled, graceful, creative, and powerful bodies in performance is an abidingly great pleasure.

We wouldn't make that claim about music or theater or any other creative activity—no one would argue that the kid playing guitar in her basement is good, but when she gets paid to play onstage it is debased and corrosive. We absolutely, unequivocally have to talk about the contours of high-performance economics, the nature of spectacle, the outrageous exploitations embedded in the sporting world, the total bullshit inequities, the way arena logics are maiming cities: all of that is exactly what I think taking sports seriously requires. But we cannot have those conversations if we do not take *all of it* seriously, and with serious respect.

I'm *not* suggesting that sports and other forms of creative expression that we claim as "art" are directly equivalent. In the same way that activists and theorists have blown the doors off high and low arts distinctions, I want to expand our definitions of creative expression. These distinctions and the bourgeois judgements that follow in their wake become murky quickly: where's the line between rhythmic gymnastics (ostensibly sport) and ballroom dancing (art) for example? Or the sport of figure skating and art of ballet? There are minor differences that become greater with other examples (say football and sculpture), but I do think it's useful to place all of it on a continuum of creative expression, with varying and shifting relationships to competition, and imbue all of it with relevance and potentiality.

Who and what has defined "sport" and "art" is helpful in understanding the trajectory, and that's a conversation I am going to return to later in a little more depth, but let me just note that those are not absolute categories, and the definitions are wholly constructed. As Louis Menand writes, talking about the 2012 Summer Games:

> Twenty-six sports will be played ... with medals awarded in three hundred and two events. The majority of those medals will be given in sports that originated, in their modern form, in Britain: archery, athletics (track and field), boxing, badminton, field hockey, football (soccer), rowing, sailing, swimming, water polo, table tennis, and tennis. Britain is also the birthplace of curling, cross-country, cricket, croquet, golf, squash, and rugby—which is scheduled to become an Olympic sport in 2016. No other country comes close. Three Olympic sports originated in the United States: basketball, volleyball, and the triathlon, which was invented in 1974. Two originated in Germany: handball and gymnastics.[8]

It's not too much of a stretch to think of modern sports (Olympic and otherwise) as the (spectacularly) monetized performance and promulgation of empire.

This is essentially true of most contemporary sports. Certain competitions seem to be timeless: who can run the fastest, lift the heaviest thing, walk the furthest along a log, etc. But what turns games into sports is standardization so that people can compete against one another using common measurements. Throwing a stick as far as you can is a game, but it's the sport of javelin when the field and stick are standardized. The invention, regulation, and bureaucratization

---

8   Louis Menand, "Glory Days," *New Yorker*, August 6th, 2012. Thanks are due here as well to Olympic historian Bill Mallon who helped me clarify some issues and aided me in my research.

of specific games as sport, however, has not happened willy-nilly or outside political and cultural contexts: the definitions, regulation, discipline, dissemination, and uses of sport have often been bent to racialist and heteronormative, masculine ends. Asking why sports are so militaristically designed, or why speed and strength are valued so much as opposed to say, rhythm and balance, is something like asking why colonialists have felt compelled to impose their wills and worldviews on the rest of the globe.

Similarly, art has always claimed to civilize, and certain forms of creativity rarely make the cut, getting relegated to "folk" or "primitive" art, or "craft" status, or just derided. Much of the art world's historically aspirational flaunt is a Cartesian prejudice for mind over body, and soul over mind. That's why "art" claims to elevate us, to lift us out of our corporal and sensual lives, with all the deeply problematic metaphysical assumptions and epistemologies that infers. Sports can turn those elitist presumptions back on themselves and insist that materialist collisions, bodies-on-bodies interactions, are where everyday politics is played out, understood, and contested. It is a primary site for apprehending who we are, how we get along with other people who may be very different from ourselves, and what ethical grounds we ascribe to.

I also think we can ask more of sports than just straight rabble-rousing. There is a constituency of political fans who view sports instrumentally, pointing to specific incidents, athletes or events as progressive flashpoints—like the Los Suns, Mahmoud Abdul-Rauf, Billie Jean King, or Muhammad Ali getting stripped of his title. Those, and so many others like them, are super-important for sure—galvanizing moments, and icons to rally around and incite the imagination. But only seeing the specific seems an inadequate rendition of politics to me. Sports matter in-and-of-themselves, not just because of how they might be leveraged.

We should be singing the praises, trumpeting, and defending any and every athlete who stands up, whether it's Jackie Robinson, John Carlos, Brittney Griner, or the kid who comes out to her high school field hockey team: that shit takes real bravery and a consistency of courage. Because sports are so volatile and so powerful, every impact reverberates something fierce. Think of the battles that ensue when a young woman just wants to play on a boy's football team, let alone the shit storm Ali caused. It's said, and I think maybe it's true, that the money shot for queer rights will be when a revered currently-playing athlete in a major sport comes out. Jason Collins probably isn't high-profile enough to fit that bill, but maybe. Magic Johnson might well have been the tipping point that finally undermined HIV/AIDS prejudices.

But leave that aside for a minute. Politics is more than iconic events or star-struck moments. You can't participate in or spectate sports without constantly articulating values, running into difference, talking about what matters and why, and being forced to figure out who you have responsibility for and why. Our core political ideals are always being performed in the gym, rink, ring, field, or track and then tested materially and bodily.

Grappling with a neoliberal era necessarily means confronting what matters. Late capitalism relentlessly reduces everything to commodity. Everyone is market fodder and everywhere is a potential profit center: nothing really matters so much that it cannot be bought and sold. Resisting neoliberalism requires us to imagine, carve out, and create non-market spaces where social and cultural relationships are animated by incommensurability. I submit that sports can be joyful, powerful, and sweet, but a whole lot more than that too.

CHAPTER TWO:

A PUNCHER'S CHANCE

AUTHENTICITY, IM/MATERIALITY, AND PHYSICALITY

It's Friday night. I'm standing ringside, a plastic cup of Michelob in hand. It's a low-end casino and I'm watching live Mixed Martial Arts. Two sweat-slicked fighters are grappling ten feet away. Remnants of smoke-machine-distributed atmosphere drift through the air. There's a posse of G-string-and-silicon ring-girls with model postures and tolerant expressions to my left. The front rows are full of lethal-looking Russian dudes with bored platinum dates, thuggy steroid users, playas, playa wannabes, and a ton of young men straight outta Jersey Shore outtakes. It's been a good evening of fights but there haven't been any really devastating knockouts yet. A couple of guys have gotten dropped hard but nothing huge. I'm a little disappointed.

But honestly, who do I think I am? I'm bald, go to the gym, and have tattoos, so I fit in here, at least at first glance. But I don't own any Affliction gear, I only make gangsta hand symbols when I'm goofing around for photos, and I haven't thrown a real punch at anyone in twenty years. I have my tough-guy affectations, but I'm a middle-aged father, I subscribe to the *New Yorker*, I drink tea, I garden. I'm out of my league here and kind of thrilled about it.

It's not just testosterone that's gotten me down here though: I'm intrigued by the explosion of interest in Mixed Martial Arts fighting. MMA carries a lugnut kind of visage, and that's part of it for sure, but it's really just an amalgam of other disciplines, infused with the admirable qualities of judo, jiu jitsu, boxing, wrestling, kickboxing, samba, and lots else. I can't see any reason to think of MMA as significantly different than any other fighting styles, aside from its current commercialization. That's part of why I am here tonight—though maybe it's because I want a taste of something real. Not "real" in the phenomenological sense: I'm talking about the right-here-right-now-in-my-face sensuality sense.

It's worth saying that I like to fight and I admire fighters of all kinds, but my goal here isn't to defend fighting per se. Instead, my defense of fighting in this context is intended to serve as a route to my larger argument about the value, power, and potentiality of *sports*, and, even more than that, the exigency of neighborly friendship. But talking about fighting provokes people, so it's a convenient way to put the argument to a stiff test right off the hop.

What I'm articulating here is an aesthetic desire for sure, but it's also, and maybe moreso, a political one. I am convinced that sports offer a particular and irreplaceable arena for radical social transformation. All sports—fighting maybe more immediately than most—open up specific and enigmatic possibilities for engaging with pillars of liberatory politics: difference, equity, and solidarity. And, in part, it's the encounter with materiality that I am after here.

It's like the difference between walking and driving: sliding by in a vehicle you really don't see shit. You can't smell or hear anything, you move too fast, you miss all the subtleties by keeping at a comfortable distance. If you walk (and especially if you walk regularly), you feel places differently. There is something analogous about the physicality, the bodies-on-bodies immediacy and pleasure of sports: it's the promise of an unmediated capacity to apprehend ethical decisions, the expression of difference, and the visceral encounters with solidarity that interest me.

THEY'RE RUNNING UP THE SCORE ON US

I've always been a fight fan. I remember watching a little black and white TV with my dad, and loving Ali sparring with Howard Cosell during prime time. I can mentally replay Hearns-Hagler in omnicolor detail. The Hit Man almost decapitating Roberto Duran. The Hawk. Alexis Arguello. Lights Out Toney. In college I was legitimately (and probably justifiably) embarrassed by my admiration of Mike Tyson and my sparring sessions in the basement of the university athletic complex. Righteous friends and nice college kids took it as proof of my loutish tendencies, so I snuck off to the north end of town on fight nights to watch pay-per-view in biker bars, trained quietly, and kept that shit right to myself. I only ever fought a little and haven't done it properly for almost two decades now, but remain enthused and attached.

And I'm not embarrassed about it anymore. I'm more confident in articulating why boxing is a good thing and why I watch. And I don't really mind so much if good people think I'm a bit of a pig. To me boxing specifically, and fighting in general, is an increasingly precious route to cut through the artifice and banality of contemporary life.

In a twenty-first century where what's real, what's fake, and what the difference is seems tenuous at best, fighting is a simple, pure pleasure. In the face of a plague of reality TV, WMDs, Facebook "friends," "conversations" on Twitter, Second Life, and the average kid spending almost eight hours a day staring at screens, looking for "reality" and "truthfulness" is a disorienting mess. Pining for the authentic mostly just sounds nostalgic, trite, and/or painfully quaint. But there's nothing fake about a sharp right cross in the mouth. There's no irony, no subtext, no spin, no fabrication, no "reality" in quotes, no disclaimers, no reset function, no replaceable avatar to start over with. It just hurts. And if you're watching, there's no way to pretend it's not happening. That kid's nose really is pouring blood, his neurons really are scrambling.

But wait. That's exactly the *Fight Club* story. Didn't Pitt and Norton and Palahniuk do all this already? Isn't the idea that fighting is particularly "authentic" just another lame Maileresque, patriarchal cliché? Really, what's real about scrapping? And what's so great about "real" or "authentic" anyways?

At first glance, I'd say it's pain, the threat of pain, the inescapable physicality that sharpens a poignancy in fighting. It has always been the ostensible realness of boxing that attracted me—I don't think boxing has anything to do with violence. Violence is coercive by definition; it's done to someone against their will. You step into the ring voluntarily. It's painful, risky, dangerous, scary, often damaging, and probably not a great idea on balance, but it's not violence. Capitalism generalizes intrinsic and extrinsic violence throughout our social and cultural relationships, and boxing is one more site for that expression. The act of fighting is scary, thrilling, and potentially damaging absolutely, but the same can be said for ballet, skateboarding, mountain climbing, scuba diving, riding a horse, mountain biking, and playing hockey. There is danger in varying degrees inhered in nearly every activity, risks to be taken and compromises to be made. Everything has a cost. If you don't like boxing, if it makes you squeamish, if you think that's not a risk you're comfortable with, I totally understand. But that's an aesthetic choice.

Well-earned physical pain and suffering, whether it's from grappling, walking all day, or digging dirt is sweet relief for those of us who sit on our asses too much, and that materiality promises an encounter with trust and solidarity. Maybe that's why I'm standing ringside after a long, immobile day writing emails, finishing an article, and applying for a grant. I'm vertical, and there are real people, real sounds, and real action around me. There is a physical encounter here that's soaking into the immateriality of my day. There is immediacy, instead of a-temporality. It's right here in front of me, and I flinch as a young man gets his elbow dislocated.

A more just and equitable world is one where we are willing to encounter the consequences of our actions and make ethical individual and collective choices. Capitalism insists that it is reasonable for an old-growth watershed to be sacrificed or workers to be downsized or land to be colonized in the name of growth and efficiency. A better world requires us being able to resist that logic and claim that some things are incommensurable: they do not adhere to market logic.

If we abandon or condescend to sports, we lose a valuable and fertile route to a world where people are more than industrial inputs: a world where people can trust and rely on each other. Sports are hardly the only way we can bodily encounter trust, but they are a specific and irreplaceable one, in no small part due to their physicality. Fighting, like all sports, requires trust, without which larger notions of solidarity and community are impossible. Why is it that after almost every bout combatants gratefully and effusively hug each other, check to make sure each other is alright, and give thanks that no one was really hurt?

The immediacy of these physical encounters forces us to face the consequences of our actions, putting our ethical choices into living color. Every time you agree to fight someone, you are placing a huge amount of trust and faith in them. There is the very real possibility that they can damage you, maybe badly. In any fight, you have to take care of the other, and pull up before anything ugly happens: you have to believe that when you tap they're going to stop. Sometimes it doesn't work. Sometimes that trust is misplaced. Overwhelmingly, though, that trust is validated. In team sports there is another layer of mutual aid involved, when you not only enter a series of agreements with your opponents, but with your teammates as well.

WITHIN STRIKING DISTANCE

The lived experience of giving and granting trust is a precondition for mutuality, or in a more abstracted, politicized rendition: solidarity. There are lots of other places to encounter this kind of mutuality, say doing work with others, but sports are one highly accessible and joyful route. Trust is necessarily bound up with the possibility of suffering, and in an antiseptic and duplicitous era, that's an attractive commodity to many—ergo the phenomenon of fake memoirs. James Frey's *A Million Little Pieces* is the flag-bearer for this genre—but there is a boatload of these clowns. Frey is a rich-kid frat boy who claimed a life of unbelievable drug and alcohol abuse, violence, Mafia relationships, and general chaos so extreme that it turned his "memoir" into a critically-lauded bestseller. Pretty much none of it was true and he got famously flogged for it.

But he is hardly alone. Over the course of multiple celebrated Oprah appearances, and in a book intended for publication in 2009 (but cancelled), Herman Rosenblat claimed that he met his wife through the fence at Buchenwald. He actually is a concentration camp survivor, but his love story and many details of his book are fantasy. In 2008, Margaret Seltzer, a rich, white suburban girl pawned off *Love and Consequences,* a memoir of growing up as a half-white and half-Native foster child, living a bad-ass life of drugs and violence as a Blood gang member. She even faked a thug accent in radio interviews, until she was exposed and the book pulled.

Then there's the weirdness of JT LeRoy who has written a bunch of books, articles, and screenplays as a once-homeless, transgender, sex-working, oft-abused drug addict. But LeRoy is a middle-aged straight woman named Laura Albert who was eventually outed (and now sued) after a long investigation. Michael Gambino published *The Honored Society* in 2001, pretending to be a full-on Mafiosa who spent significant time in jail for murder, pimping, money laundering and all the rest. None of it was true. In 1997, Misha Defonseca wrote a massive European bestseller about being a Holocaust survivor, killing a German soldier, and living with a pack of wolves (!). It was B.S. In 1995, Binjamin Wilkomirski wrote a similar Holocaust survival story that was hugely popular and won plenty of literary awards. Also total B.S.

There are tons of other examples of memoir-deception, both recent and historical, many of them prominent hoaxes. The thread that runs through these stories is the presumption of authenticity in describing a life of trauma and pain. These fake memoirs are all characterized by their "gritty realism" and their witness to "horrifying reality." A huge proportion of fake memoirs are written by people pretending to be indigenous or Holocaust survivors.

Nasdijj, for example, wrote three acclaimed and awarded books, starting with 2000's *The Blood Runs Like A River Through My Dreams*, about growing up Navajo, his brutal childhood and abusive parents, eventually adopting an FAS kid, then an HIV+ child. *Esquire* reviewed it as an "authentic, important book.... Unfailingly honest and very nearly perfect." Except it was a total lie. He's a white guy from Michigan named Tim Barrus.

All these books claimed authenticity on the basis of suffering. Misery lit is a boom sector of the flailing publishing world, and from Frank McCourt to Dave Pelzer to Augusten Burroughs, offering up personal grief has made for good business, so it's hardly any wonder that a few folks with less-than-traumatic lives have given it their best shot, reality notwithstanding.

It's not just books either. Memoir is a fluid genre, and much of the hiphop I listen to is predicated on streetness. I love 50 Cent, but how would I feel if all his bravado and macho bullshit was a total lie? *He got shot like I got shot but he ain't fuckin' breathing*. I presume that thug rappers are habitually full of shit about their heroics, but at least I know it's coming and love them for it. I don't mind too much when my hiphop bleeds fiction and non-fiction a little: talking trash is part of the package. But I made no such deals with Frey before I read a *Million Little Pieces* and most everybody hates being lied to. Including Sherman Alexie, who isn't real fond of Nasdijj either: "His lies matter because he has cynically co-opted as a literary style the very real suffering endured by generations of very real Indians because of very real injustices caused by very real American aggression that destroyed very real tribes."[1]

But why is pain so identified with authenticity? And vice versa? Why is street cred about the suffering you've endured? In a world buried in half-truths and untruths, in lust with artifice and superficiality, a life watched on screen, what's with the hand-wringing about realness? Is fighting really more authentic than sitting at my computer all day?

---

1   *Time Magazine*, February 6, 2006.

Why is pain more real than pleasure? Is it that pain is a documentable affirmation of consequence?

That's more or less what is going through my mind as I consider how to extract myself from a kimura submission hold that Roy Duquette has put me in. A kimura is a jiu jitsu hold, more or less the same as a hammerlock, chicken-wing, or *ude-garami*. It also fucking hurts. Roy's in side control and is hyper-rotating my shoulder by pinning my chest and leveraging my upper and lower arms in opposite directions.

Roy's a good guy. He is a trainer, coach, and therapist who works with all kinds of fighters at all kinds of levels including stars like Dennis Kang from the UFC and Emily Kwok, who in 2007 became the first female Canadian to win a world championship in Brazilian jiu jitsu. Roy has trained in a bouquet of disciplines himself including jiu jitsu, boxing, grappling, Karate, and Russian Sambo, and still spars regularly. He knows what he's doing.

We've sat and talked at length about his philosophies of fighting and I've watched him train and spar several times. He employs a melange of styles, but not haphazardly. Roy is a classic new-school MMA practitioner: it's not meathead bar-brawl stuff he employs, it's more like chess with submissions. Roy is convinced that there is something elemental about fighting, especially martial arts, mixed or otherwise: "There's no hiding when you're fighting. That's the realness of it—it's an expression of you."

Sure, but I think that's really true about hockey or dancing too. You learn so much about someone just by playing a little pick-up ball or baling hay or cleaning a house with them. It's not easy to hide yourself on the court or when doing hard work with someone. Roy tells me,

> That's exactly what I teach my students: to be connected to your opponent. If you can't get

into a relationship with your opponent you're already in trouble. You have to focus completely. No matter what happened to you that day you have to leave it behind. In that way we could say that what happens outside the ring is *less* real than what happens in it.

Today I've convinced him to work with me a little, just for fun. I think I'm strong enough and I like to fight, but I have no idea what I am doing. I have no wrestling or grappling skills, but I'm game and excited to learn some jiu jitsu.

Roy also brings along a student of his: Emma Lynds, a thirty-six-year-old mother of two who is the only woman owner of a martial arts gym in Vancouver. She also has a black-belt in Hapkido and trains extensively in muay thai, boxing, judo, and jiu jitsu. The three of us take turns fighting over the next couple of hours. Roy and Emma are beautiful to watch: spinning, rolling, leaping over each other, countering, counter-countering, and countering again. Roy has a lot more jiu jitsu experience and is far bigger than Emma so he wears her down every time, but there's no charity going on, he has to fight hard.

I love fighting with Emma. She's 135 pounds and I can muscle her around, but she is so smart and skilled that I am constantly getting caught in holds that are very difficult for me to negotiate out of. Because I am fifty pounds heavier, Emma works from her back keeping me in full-guard most of the time. In our first bout, she just fends me off patiently for a few minutes, then locks in a triangle choke that finishes things. In our next few rounds, I figure out a couple of moves so I have some offense. Emma is really helpful, waiting as Roy pauses us and explains what I should be doing, and letting me try stuff out. It feels like I am in a fight, even though I know Emma could submit me pretty easily. Her conditioning is awesome, while I wear down quickly, which clouds my thinking. It's really Emma's quick reactions and strategic manoeuvring that impresses me most.

Fighting with Roy is another deal. He just toys with me as I flail around. He repeatedly takes about thirty seconds to get me in some horrific situation that I have to bail out of immediately, and often it's a lot faster than that. I tap out of the kimura and try again. I shoot at Roy's legs with some conviction, but he splays backwards effortlessly with his elbows on the back of my neck driving my face into the mat. I roll over quickly, but he's on me again. I spin and get to all fours, thinking something good might happen, but before I can figure out what that might be I'm in an anaconda choke that I have completely failed to defend against. I drop down and pull at his forearms but Roy just bears down on me. This is only going to end poorly, so I tap again. I think Roy's just going through a catalog of classic MMA submission moves as a kind of encyclopaedic lesson: he's working his way down the list. It doesn't seem to matter what I try—he just keeps schooling me.

It's all good though. It's comforting that we're doing this without the threat of punches, elbows, and/or knees raining down on my face. And it's really fun hanging out in someone else's world, especially when they are as skilled and generous as Roy and Emma. I commit to coming back more consistently. Aside from the occasional burst of shooting pain and the promise of a stiff neck tomorrow, I feel like I am in the moment, like I am really present; I have to be, actually. The experience is literally in my face. I'm no Buddhist, but that idea of presence, of actually *being there* makes sense to me.

TALKING A GOOD GAME

A few days after grappling with Roy and Emma, with my shoulders still shooting with pain whenever I lift my arms too high above my head, I decided to try another tack and called up Gabe Forsythe looking to play some video games. Gabe's another great guy. He's a smart kid: the media education coordinator at an arty rep cinema downtown and he runs a whole variety of video production and media literacy programs in schools. He also owns an X-Box 360, so I figured he could help me out.

Gabe and I eat dinner and talk vids for a while, then we start with *NHL '12*. I am shocked at the veracity of the game. The players look startlingly like actual NHLers, the movements are subtle and complex, even the built-in play-by-play commentary is amazingly accurate. The complexity of the game is even more stunning. There are a dizzying array of options and game choices, including the X-Box "Live" function, which allows Gabe to get online and play with and against up to twelve players from all over the world, including talking real-time trash on their headsets.

I am totally intimidated—fuck, this is no Pac-Man—so I let Gabe play while I barrage him with questions. He plays and I watch for a half-hour, then we switch over to *Call Of Duty IV: Modern Warfare*. If *NHL '12* was overwhelming, I don't know what the hell to say about *COD4*. It is so realistic, so sophisticated, so incredibly fast, so totally disorienting that I kind of panic and pee myself a little when I try to play. The controllers have like 700 functions: two little joysticks, a four-clover little assemblage of color-coded buttons, two right and two left trigger-things that can be single or double-pumped to various effect.

The action is sonic-fast, unrelenting, and multi-dimensional. Gabe sets an avatar and chooses an assemblage weapons, levels, and scenarios from about a billion options. He plays for a while on Live, with dozens of players occupying what looks to be a destroyed Serbian village battlefield, all of them careening around firing, knifing, sub-machining, stun-bombing, grenading, and calling in air strikes on each other. It is total mayhem. Gabe dies repeatedly, constantly, often using the replay function to see who the hell just offed him and from where. When he hands me the reins I am laughably incompetent. Just getting my guy to run through the starting house, shoot a few targets, and slide down a rope is brutal and takes me fifteen minutes to figure out. And that's playing by myself. The actual game is a gong show on my part. Let's not get into it here.

The experience of playing fighting video games could hardly be more different than fighting. After a few hours of vids I feel disembodied, buzzed, spaced out, and totally irritable. I feel the opposite of "present." It was a lot of fun hanging out with Gabe, but I feel like I just killed off four hours of my life that I'm never going to get back. But maybe that's just cliché. Maybe video games are just something I'm a total rookie at, and thus spooked. Maybe I could get used to playing COD and find some kind of rhythm to settle into.

There is certainly tons of skill involved in playing video games, I can see how it might be fun and it doesn't seem particularly anti-social. In fact, Gabe talks at length—and convincingly, too—about the social aspects of gaming, both playing with his local buddies and especially the friends he has made playing Live. He regularly gathers online with a group of guys who live in Vegas to play hockey. Gabe can find them easily, knows them by name, and the group has an easy familiarity and respect for each other. But the Live gaming relationship strikes me as weirdly dystopic ... or is it just unfamiliar?

Without question, there is something clearly, viscerally different about the two experiences. It feels like the distance between sunshine and a light box. But why is physical fighting "real" and online fighting not? Is one set of feelings—one visceral, immediate, and physical, the other abstract, removed, and imaginary—more authentic than the other? Isn't fighting just as manufactured and constrained as gaming, just a little more physical (and even

that only in specific ways)? I think calling physical fighting *authentic* and simulated fighting *fake* is highly dubious.
Actually, I suspect that those are *precisely* the wrong set of
questions to ask: that searching for the "real" is a ruse. We
need to be asking what matters, what is worth preserving,
and what is worth protecting.

THAT'S A CLOWN QUESTION, BRO[2]

A fixation with authenticity is not a recent phenomenon,
but in our post-modern world it seems to have acquired
new contours and nuances. To consider this, I equipped
myself as I tend to do (and maybe a little ironically), by
looking for some books to help me think it through. As I
exited the library in downtown Vancouver, I pulled over for
a coffee at a swanky little spot. It's tucked artfully between
steel and glass towers, backgrounded by a wall of satellite
dishes from the CBC compound.

I am attracted to the place because it is a little wood
building, designed beautifully to look like a shack in the
woods, if styled by an urban eco-architect. It grasps at
authenticity in the midst of artifice. The low slanting roof
is covered with tufty little plants and grasses and there a
lovely, burnished wood patio area. It's not really a café,
more of a take-out joint, but the interior is equally styl-
ized: the design references are all urban loft, with cracked
concrete floors with a shiny bronzed sheen, steel counters,
a sort of restrained, industrial décor, big windows. Even the
take-out paper cups are designed within an inch of their
lives, adorned with East Van-esque artwork lending a gritty
but tasteful edge to the caffeinating experience. Everything
this company does is carefully constructed to confirm their
claims to urban authenticity.

As I leave with my coffee, blinking in the sun, I almost
bump into an enormous dude, who I suspect is Samoan,

---

2   Famously spoken by Bryce Harper in June 2012.

on the sidewalk. I watch him roll past, long dreads hanging down his back. The dreads are perfect: all of equal length, equal roundness, equal tidiness. In fact, they look fake— actually I'm pretty sure they are extensions—and I (very!) privately scoff. What a dork. Extensions? *C'mon.*

But really, what's with my derisiveness? So what if they're extensions? Does it make him less real? I guess he bought the hair instead of committing to the years it would take to grow them, and I don't hold any particular regard for folks who take deep pleasure and interest in their own hair. But how are dude's extensions any different than my "distressed" jeans? I bought these at H&M, specially designed to look worn-in, creased, faded in the right spots. I bought them for that authentic jeans look.

The problem here isn't really the ostentatious bullshit of that café, my jeans, or the guy's extensions. It's the fact that my pants were made by vastly underpaid and underrespected women in Bangladesh that's the problem. It's where the hair came from to make those extensions. It's who picked these coffee beans and how much they got paid. It's the conun- drums of remix culture in a time where everything, every bit of creativity, is in play, whether it's sampling or fusing someone else's hair with yours. This is exactly where the confluences of real and not, artifice and materiality, owner- ship and open source, exploitation and homage muddy the waters when we try to make sense of what matters.

I spent the last two hours listening to Lil Wayne mix tapes, cut and diced, on a free download site, then switched over to a Johnny Cash remix. Just like Cash borrowed profligately from Hank Williams, the Texas Playboys, and Jimmy Rodgers, hip-hop sampling and remixing extends the notion that all culture rests on plagiarism. It's what all culture does and has always done: borrowed, cut, pasted, moved, and shifted. Calling something "authentic" pre- supposes an original source, reifies it, calcifies it, and then evaluates all other renditions by how close they replicate that imaginary Adam and Eve.

Consider Brian Jungen. He's a brilliant Vancouver artist who makes beautiful masks out of Nike Air Jordans. They're fabulous pieces: totally traditional and entirely unorthodox. As he puts it: "by simply manipulating the Air Jordan shoes you could evoke specific cultural traditions whilst simultaneously amplifying the process of cultural corruption and assimilation. The Nike mask sculptures seemed to articulate a paradoxical relationship between a consumerist artifact and an 'authentic' native artefact."[3]

How about Jungen? Are his masks "inauthentic"? Does it matter that he is of Swiss and Dunne-za First Nations heritage? It sure as hell does. If white-boy mongrel me was making and selling native masks made out of sneakers we would be having a different conversation. All culture is collage, nostalgia is always lazy, and none of are us are authentic: we're all synthetic hybrids and that's all good. But who is borrowing what from whom is always important, and lying, appropriation, and stealing always matter. Culture, like gender, is performance, and it is high time we ditch the idea of authenticity, stop looking for the "real" and start talking about the "good."

I am arguing for the opposite of a relativist cultural stance here. I don't want a flight away from politics, but rather an embrace of it. We live in a distracted, evasive, artificial, facile world with our lives increasingly reduced to digital communication and virtual relationships, and we cannot keep trying to default to an imaginary, pre-established authenticity, or deferring to an inevitable determinism. Judgment doesn't exist somewhere outside of us: ethics and politics are our responsibility.

But this is exactly the problem we're faced with: in a neoliberal landscape divorced from living and breathing

---

3   See http://en.wikipedia.org/wiki/Brian_Jungen.

consequences, the possibility of those conversations—the possibilities of debate and contention about what matters—are inherently undermined. In this slippery, pain-renouncing world, arguments flourish (obviously), but when profoundly abstracted from the world of bodies and stuff, who really gives a fuck? Just keep moving. Politicized conversations about ideas like friendship, generosity, solidarity, or hospitality have little value in a world that disdains pain and trust. We need to find ways talk about good and bad, right and wrong, useful and destructive, ennobling or reducing.

And that gets me back to sports. I'm not overwhelmingly compelled by the MMA myself nor do I want you to become a fan of jiu jitsu or boxing or any kind of fighting really. But I *do* want you to respect it, and respect the possibilities of all sports. I'm glad to be standing ringside not because it's real, or an authentic experience, but because it has lived consequence, because it's like a cool drink of water on a hot day, an everyday performance of trust and neighborliness. A better world has to be able to antagonize the neoliberal logic of a one-world 24/7 marketplace where everything and everyone is subsumed into a consumptive, commodified landscape: and here, in the face of body-on-body contact, I can see something else at play.

I am interested in a world where land, housing, food, and labor cannot be profited from. Exploitation (in both senses) is written into the DNA of capitalism, but neoliberalism requires that the consequences of our actions be obscured from us. We do not care particularly that our cell phones and computers are powered by coltan and brutal child labor in the Congo. Our relentless transcontinental flying is contributing profoundly to climate change but that alters very few of our vacation plans. Each of our consumer products contains and obscures a whole range of social relations, many of them atrocious, but I still want those jeans.

Sports offers an arena to cut through that haze. The social relations in sports tend to be right there and available, the implications and repercussions of individual actions impossible to obscure. All too often, that means looking at the ugliest parts of our culture in a cold, fluorescent glare, but even that's got a silver(ish) lining: at least we can see that ugliness straight up. At other times and in other places, there is genuine opportunity and undeniable opportunities for shift.

CHAPTER THREE:

CHIPPING AWAY
AT A BIG LEAD

BODIES OF WORK,
GENDER, AND SEX

There's nowhere better to learn if you're a real man or a sissy than by playing sports. Want to know if your dick is big enough? Spend time in a locker room (FYI—it's not). Hey ladies: want to learn if you're too butch, your legs are too big, your shoulders too cut? Anyone up for having their sexuality challenged and/or debased? How about getting a full-frontal blast of heteronormativity? Want to spend time somewhere queerphobic or just plain hateful rhetoric gets tossed around casually? Feel like getting a good taste of Neanderthal sexual politics?

If you're up for any of that I highly recommend the sporting world. Start playing, or even better start watching TV. Any given Sunday is a good beginning. Where else is normative masculinity/femininity enforced with such enthusiasm as in the sports world? Where else can you encounter shit you were sure left the civilized world decades ago? Where else can you be comfortably assured you will encounter distasteful, hostile, and/or very possibly violent thinking and behavior based on the shape of people's bodies and their choice of partners?

Whether it's the stands, field, locker room, television, Internet, floor, or rink, there is a long-standing tradition that threads through almost every sport, which stabilizes and reinforces dominant and dominating notions of what it means to be a man or a boy, a woman or a girl, and what the distinctions should be between them. Often those conversations are cloaked in supposedly ethical, jock-culture, character-building, cliché-ridden separating-the-men-from-the-boys, bullshit dogma that only barely hides presumptive notions of how you should look and act, and sneers at those who don't conform, labelling them as physically, and thus morally, weak.

As I've test-run the arguments in this book with friends and family, the first response of many is to point to the hideous sexual and gender politics so endemic to so many sports. And of course there's no denying it. But look again from another perspective and very often there is something else going on too: think Billie Jean King, Emile Griffith, Gareth Thomas, David Testo, Martina Navratilova, Greg Louganis, Sheryl Swoopes, Donal Óg Cusack, John Amaechi, Jason Collins. Think Renee Richards.[1] Think of

---

1   In an earlier draft of this book, my editor Kate Khatib wrote me a note: "I just want to point out that I have no idea who just about any of these people are. Rattling off a list of names that are completely meaningless to non-sports fans is probably not the best approach." I agreed with her, and then noticed that I do that a lot in this book—rattle off lists of names that will mean something to some people, but for others (specifically to those who aren't huge fans) it might come off as snobby or alienating. So I went back

all the incipient and demanding, subtle and overt challenges to traditional notions of femininity that women athletes raise just by playing.

BRINGING OUR A-GAME

Or, think of someone like Brian Burke. In lots of ways dude
is your prototypical hockey a-hole: a big, constantly pug-
nacious, gruff, ruddy-faced poser who spits out tough-guy
hockey clichés like teeth after a good fight. He's so full of
bluster and bullshit it's hard to take him seriously, but I
kind of love the guy.

Burke (or Burkie, if you like, in the hockey vernacu-
lar) was a good U.S. college hockey player who made it
to the (minor-league, pro) AHL where he played a year,
then bailed out and went to Harvard Law School. After
he graduated in 1981 he became a player agent then got
a front office job with the Vancouver Canucks then in
1992 became the GM of the Hartford Whalers. He left
the job after a year to become an Executive VP for the
NHL head office, where he stayed until returning to
Vancouver in 1998 as GM of the Canucks. After rebuild-
ing that team significantly, he was let go in 2004, then
was named GM of the Anaheim Ducks, where they won
a Stanley Cup in 2007. The next year, Burke left that
post to become the GM and President of the Toronto

---

and tried to fix it, in part because I totally want to speak directly
to non-fans here. But I couldn't really make it work! I tried putting
in footnotes explaining everyone, but that was clunky and boring
as shit to read. I tried taking the lists out, but it really butchered
the flow and I lost something important. I tried contextualizing the
lists narratively, but it seemed cumbersome and also boring. So, I
just ended up leaving the lists in. As K8 notes, if you don't recognize the names you are probably not going to look them up (in part
because I drop so many of them) and I understand that I might lose
a few of you there. Sorry about that.

Maple Leafs,[2] a job he held until early 2013 when he got axed again.

Burke is as much a "hockey-guy" silverback as you could possibly find. He's spent his life as a player, agent, league exec, general manager, and TV commentator. He's famous for his combative personal style, his aggressiveness with the media, and his strong and often hostile opinions. The guy constantly looks like he just left a brawl but is ready—and eager—to drop the gloves again, right now if need be. It's an image he clearly loves, nurtures, and polishes to a sheen.

It's also a style Burke brings to his hockey teams. As he described his hopes for the Maple Leafs: "We require, as a team, proper levels of pugnacity, testosterone, truculence and belligerence. That's how our teams play. I make no apologies for that. Our teams play a North American game. We're throwbacks. It's black-and-blue hockey … The first thing and probably the easiest thing to change on your team is the amount of the snarl, the amount of the bite."[3]

So maybe it was a surprise and maybe it wasn't that when his son Brendan came out as gay to his family in 2007 and publicly in 2009, Burke immediately and openly backed him with the same aggressiveness. Brendan had quit playing hockey in high school, worried that he would be ostracized by his teammates if they discovered his sexuality, but by the time he was attending Miami University (in Ohio) had decided to pursue a career in hockey and was serving as the varsity team's video coordinator manager. After coming out to his teammates and fellow coaches, he was greeted with wide support from the team, university, and fans.

---

2   Although the Leafs have been consistently atrocious for forty-five years, they remain the league's most valuable team and arguably its most prominent/iconic franchise.

3   Paul Hunter, "Burke Promises More Leaf Toughness," *Toronto Star*, November 30, 2008.

Soon his story became highly public with feature stories on ESPN, TSN, newspapers, and sites across the continent, and Brendan was often interviewed, sometimes with his father, who unequivocally backed him. In the TSN interview, Brian was asked if he thought the NHL was ready for an openly gay player, scout, executive, or coach, and his answer was, "They are welcome in the Toronto Maple Leafs organization … and I have to guess we're not alone."[4]

Brendan, tragically, was killed in 2010 while driving in heavy snow at age twenty-one. In response, the Burke family has ramped up their advocacy for gay athletes impressively. Brian marches in the Toronto Pride Parade wearing a Maple Leafs jersey, and Brendan's brother Patrick, a scout for the Philadelphia Flyers, with support from family and friends launched the You Can Play Project in 2012, an organization devoted to "ensuring equality, respect and safety for all athletes, without regard to sexual orientation."

One of their core initiatives has been to produce a series of PSAs featuring current hockey players articulating their support for LGBT issues, and their respect for teammates and fans regardless of orientation. As Brian put it: "Young gay athletes are just not staying in team sports. And you know, in my mind, it's kind of a critical area to attack, it's kind of an area where the two fields don't intersect. No one ever talks about gay athletes. No one ever encourages them."[5]

The videos are great to watch. There's one player after another, ostensibly a bunch of hockey goons, standing there saying solid, cool shit: "I'm proud to be an LGBT ally," "I'm not going to be the guy who holds people back," "It's

---

4   Interview on TSN in the first period intermission of the Toronto-Tampa Bay game, Wednesday, November 25, 2009.

5   The Burke quotes here were widely reported. I lifted them from Bruce Arthur, "Patrick Burke spreads message of inclusion in memory of his brother Brendan," *National Post*, March 4, 2012.

time to change the way the world thinks about athletes," "Respect your teammates and fans no matter who they are," and on and on. There's stars like Stamkos, Lundqvist, Price, Giroux, Perry, Nash, and Keith, thugs like Parros, Weber, Clutterbuck, and Phaneuf, and lots others.

"It should do two things," Burke says. "It should validate the message, and it should empower young athletes to listen to the message.... You see Z [Boston Bruins defenseman Zdeno Chara] on camera, everyone knows who Chara is, and how tough he is, and by the way he's just a wonderful person, just a gem of a human being. And you see him, and I think it validates the message, and authenticates the message, because everyone knows who he is and everyone knows how he plays. And for him to say, 'I support the gay community and I want you to, too,' I think is a very strong message. I'm proud of the players that are doing this."[6] Burke argues that having prominent players make the argument brings it home to kids in a way no one else really could.

I think he's pretty much right. Sexuality and gender are in constant discussion on the field/ice/floor: some of it brutal, but lots of it interesting and unmistakably present. Because the field of play is so fraught, and because it is such a locus point, the fat is right in the fire. The materiality and the constant physical engagement of hockey, like all sports, forces participants and audiences alike to think intently about bodies and their uses.

Both Burke's shtick and the You Can Play Project are consistently cloaked in layers of macho B.S. about manliness and toughness and stuff (narratives, frankly, that I, myself, am highly susceptible and mostly amenable to ... as if you couldn't tell!), but let that aside for a second: there's some compelling progress here. When Patrick says it's time to "kick the fucking door down" on gay rights in sports

---

6   Ibid.

you gotta cheer. Hockey just is a tough-ass sport. And if hockey as a generalized culture actively enforces particular, dominant renditions of masculinity, that's worthy of conversation for sure, but I don't see anything wrong necessarily with valorizing toughness as a virtue.[7]

The point that I'm after here is that sports offer a uniquely fecund arena for conversations about bodies, their uses, and how we perform them. I think Burke's correct when he suggests that Zdeno Chara standing in front of a camera to support gay athletes has a discernible, irreplaceable impact. It's because of his celebrity, sure, but also because he's a big, rough guy, which is somehow supposed to refute the notion that queerness suggests an inherent lack of "toughness," whatever the hell that might mean. That's some highly problematic territory for sure, and worth "kicking the fucking door down" on too, but one step at a time. The implication that homophobia will elicit a beatdown from George Parros makes it a worthy exercise, says me, and I suspect that this really does filter down to the lived experience of everyday people playing hockey for a club team or at the community center.

A TOTAL TEAM EFFORT

I'm not sure if a major sports star coming out or openly standing for LGBT rights has *more* social impact than Ricky Martin or Ellen or whoever, but because it's a different arena with a different kind of impact and a special kind of resonance, we need to position sports as a site not just of reproduction, but of production.

I don't think there's any question that every little step towards tolerance has repercussive effects. The NHL now punishes anti-gay slurs the same way they do on-ice racist taunts, and you can be hit with a suspension for homophobic

---

7   But only so long as we continue fucking with every notion of what constitutes "tough."

language. I told my partner, Selena, about this, describing this as "kind of amazing—you can say the nastiest, vilest shit on the ice: you can drop horrible insults, talk about what you're going to do with someone's mother or sister, but drop a racist or homophobic comment and bam, suspension and derision." She looked up and said: "Good to hear misogyny is still OK. The last holdout, huh?" Yup, pretty much. And that speaks to how much more territory needs to be crossed to counter not just heteronormativity but to reimagine the constant (athletic) performance of gender and sexuality.

That's work that someone like Ben Cohen both contributes to and reinforces. Ben is kind of a hero. He's a former British pro rugby player of considerable stature, having played first division for Northampton, Brile, and the Sale Sharks, and representing England from 2000–2006, and is the tenth-highest point scorer in England rugby history and third all-time among England try scorers. Dude's also a beautiful young man who early in his career emerged as gay icon often appearing shirtless in magazines, calendars, fan sites, and more than a few fantasies. He's got the handsome friendly face and huge, cut build that is terminally and kind of comprehensively attractive.

Ben has also experienced his share of struggle. He's clinically deaf in both ears and in 2000 his father was killed while defending a patron in the pub he managed. So maybe it's a surprise and maybe not that nearing the end of his career he retired and formed the Stand Up Foundation: "the world's first foundation dedicated to raising awareness of the long-term, damaging effects of bullying, and funding those doing real-world work to stop it. We stand up against bullying regardless of to whom it happens. Because lesbian, gay, bisexual and transgender (LGBT) people are often targeted by bullies, we give particular attention to this community. We include removing homophobia from sports as central to our mission."

I'm not sure how much it matters that Ben is straight and married with two kids. Maybe to some degree. He has always been public in acknowledging his gay following and being grateful for it. He's exactly the kind of guy you want coming out in support of queer rights and especially queer rights in sports. He's badass, straight, respected, and passionate. Great guy and I suspect he's having the same kind of impact in the U.K. that You Can Play is having here in North America, and in hockey in particular.

In some ways, these struggles for access and rights, equality, fairness, and justice seem like pretty easy shots. I can't really imagine where the debate per se is, aside from the mouths of straight-up bigots. Obviously, there is a long freaking ways to go and it's hardly all sunshine, rainbows, and unicorns for women's and queer rights in society in general, and sports even more so, but the historical trajectory seems headed in the right general direction around LGBT inclusion and equal women's participation.

Consider the Yunel Escobar incident in the fall of 2012, when the Toronto Blue Jays' young Cuban shortstop inexplicably entered a game with "*Tu Ere Maricon*" written on his eyeblack. He was suspended for three games, his lost $90,000 salary was donated to GLAAD and You Can Play, and he was roundly condemned by players, fans, and owners alike. But that wasn't enough for many (most?) and the local sports talk media brayed for days afterward about how there was no place for that in the game and he should be thrown off the team pronto. It was a widespread reaction I didn't anticipate.

I know I am citing a few positive incidents here, and pointing towards a few inspiring folks, while there are god-knows how many hideous situations and real goons that I'm not talking about. That said, I feel confident in suggesting that the ship's pointed, generally speaking, in the right direction. As women's sports become incrementally mainstreamed and popularized, larger notions of femininity will surely continue to be expanded and contested. But still, pervasive sexist and misogynist attitudes persist with malicious stamina.

The ugliness that is flung towards women (of all kinds, in so many renditions), and is so tiresomely expected in the sports world requires more work than ever. There are huge battles ahead to make sports more inclusive and less hateful, but it feels to me that at least the route is clear and comprehensible. The next step I think, is to see sports as pregnant with possibilities for challenging notions of gender and to explore ideas of what bodies are supposed to look and act like, in part because when you play, watch, or talk about sports you are necessarily thinking carefully about bodies, yours and others.

And that's not something most of us are all that comfortable with. Western culture tends to deploy both revulsion and reification in the face of physical experience and labor. Technological innovation is overwhelmingly designed to obviate work, to allow us to avoid physical contact with each other or the material world. Jobs that revolve around immateriality are admired and sought far over those that require bodily labor. Rich people don't do anything for themselves, and we know we've "made it" when we don't have to cook, clean, shop, garden, or fix anything for ourselves.

At the same time, there is a reflexive ethical value attributed to labor, to working with our hands, to "real" jobs, and there's sometimes nostalgic, sometimes heart-felt faith in materiality. It's in these waters where sports swim, where the frank tangibility of bodies and their capacities are both inescapable and open for conversation. Those moments, the constant thinking about bodies and an embedded fixation on fairness and justice, are one clear line where sports extend into other arenas of life.

SEPARATING THE BOYS FROM THE MEN (AND THE BOYS FROM THE GIRLS)

The challenge that someone like Ben Cohen or Brian Burke offers is different than that of Serena Williams, Lisa Leslie, Dana Torres, Brittney Griner, Sam Stosur, Holly Mangold, or Rhonda Rousey. Each of these women, and so many more like them (both well known and not), present an alternative rendition of femininity, attractiveness, beauty, and strength, to varying kinds of effect. There's just no way to encounter women like these without having notions of womanhood tweaked just a little, and that's nothing but goodness.

But Caster Semenya presents another kind of a question, one that's simultaneously problematic and kind of thrilling in its repercussions. Semenya's is a story that a lot of people are familiar with: a young middle-distance runner from South Africa who took the track world by storm in 2009 winning the 800 meters at the World Championships with the best time posted in the world that year. She has remained at the top of her sport, winning silver at the 2012 London Olympics.

In between those two events however she was the object of intense scrutiny as her gender was repeatedly questioned. Semenya presents some markedly "masculine" characteristics: she has a solid jaw, thick muscles, and broad shoulders. She emerged on the scene quickly and made swift leaps up the performance ladder, which, in an era of endemic PED suspicions, raised reflexive eyebrows. The story really starts though after her 2009 win when the IAAF (International Association of Athletics Federations) demanded gender testing. Information about the demand and the semi-secret test was leaked and then it turned into a real shit-storm that continued through 2010.

There was a flurry of ham-handed maneuvering by the IAAF and the ASA (Athletics South Africa) sometimes confirming, sometimes denying, sometimes lying about whether or not Semenya was being tested. Then there were unanswered questions about what exactly she was being tested for and why, and what exactly her formal rights and responsibilities were. A number of athletes came to her defense (as did South Africans in general), but others were unapologetic in their belief that she had some kind of "unfair advantage."

She was barred from competing through the spring of 2010, despite official confusion on what exactly was going on and no clear confirmation what they might be testing for exactly (eventually the IAAF claimed they were not suggesting she was cheating, but that maybe she had a "rare medical condition"). Finally Semenya was allowed to run (apparently she "passed") in June of 2010 and, despite battling through some injuries, maintained world-class form and pulled off Olympic silver, carrying the South African flag in the opening ceremonies.

Many of the questions her case exposed remain, however, and three of them seem especially germane here. The first two questions are bound up with one another: Is Semenya a man or a woman? And, how would we know? The third question flows easily from there: Does she have an unfair advantage? In many ways, it is obscuring to focus on this particular case, but I think the answers have impact not just for those interested in the intersection of sports and gender, but for thinking about sports in general, and for conversations that extend further into other aspects of everyday life.

The first place to start, I'd say, is to again note that what we call sports (and what we don't) has been constructed assiduously around nationalism and colonialism (more on this in the next couple of chapters), but that, as an institution, one of sport's main narrative thrusts has always been concretizing gender. It is hard to even start thinking about sports without thinking of gender binaries: boys play here, girls over there, and the two don't mix. Sports consistently segregate men and women into two distinct categories of activity and insist that they do not cross-pollinate. In this insistence, sports works very hard to deepen our notions of how boys and girls should behave: toughens boys up, turns boys into men, and women should steer well clear.

Embedded in those kinds of threads are other claims around violence, battle, masculine citizenship, and preparing young men for war, but even a quick foray into gender theory starts to screw all that "boys will be boys" shit right up. A couple of decades of sophisticated thinking and theorizing has effectively destroyed the idea of a gender binary, and many people are now comfortable talking about a gender spectrum or continuum on which people consistently invent and reinvent they ways they perform their places. The idea of fixed male and female roles, behaviors, and trajectories is in the process of being discredited pretty thoroughly in the popular consciousness.

IT IS WHAT IT IS

Running parallel to gender is sex, and the question of whether or not we can biologically distinguish between men and women. What seems, at first glance, like a simple answer has been thrown into confusion by people like Caster Semenya. There are a significant (and perhaps wildly underestimated) number of people who do not conform to simple sex binary criteria like genitalia, hormones, chromosomes, or gonadal characteristics. There are many people who present XX / XY chromosomal diversions, others who have elevated or reduced androgen/testosterone/estrogen levels, some who have non-conforming genitalia, and still others who have combinations of all of these diversions and/or others. Many people may not have had any of these "anomalies" identified medically or even vernacularly.

An overwhelming majority of people who are born with noticeably non-conforming characteristics (like ambiguous genitalia) have surgery conducted on them at birth, with medical professionals assigning a gender to which the individual conforms accordingly. But there are other people who do not have overtly recognizable diversions, who are assigned their gender and sex via genitalia, but carry with them non-definitive characteristics that might lead to confusion, bullying, hostility, and sometimes outright discrimination and violence. This is the territory where Semenya lands: she has female genitalia but apparently some other "male" biological features and perhaps an elevated testosterone level, all of which induce a kind of gender panic, not just because of her transgressive ambiguity, but because she just fucks high-level athletics up in ways that aren't really resolvable right now.

Righteous rivals claim you can clearly tell Caster is a man "just by looking at her,"[8] while indignant defenders suggest that she is a girl because that is what she has always been assessed as: "This girl has been castigated from day one, based on what?... You denounce my child as a boy when she's a girl? If you did that to my child, I'd shoot you."[9] Obviously neither of these arguments is adequate and each really relies on a kind of gender discipline that tries to resolve "the problem" with forceful policing.

---

8   See, for example, Russian runner Mariya Savinova's comments in Robyn Dixon, "Runner Caster Semenya has heard the gender comments all her life," *Los Angeles Times*, August 21, 2009.

9   Leonard Chuene, then of the International Association of Athletic Federations (IAAF). Also widely quoted, see for example: Brenna Munro, "Caster Semenya: Gods and Monsters," *Safundi: The Journal of South African and American Studies* 11.4 (2010); Tavia Nyong'o, "The unforgivable transgression of being Caster Semenya," *Women & Performance: A Journal of Feminist Theory* 20.1 (2010); Luke Winslow, "Colonizing Caster Semenya: Gender Transformation and the Makeover Genre," *Western Journal of Communication* 76.3 (2012).

In non-sporting life it should be all fine and good for Caster to inhabit whatever gender(s) and/or sexes she feels like: there's plenty of contention, but no legitimate dispute there. The "problem" is that sports, as we currently understand them, are built around particular notions of fairness, justice, and a level playing field. They're standardized, competitive games that employ and depend upon the same set of rules and regulations anywhere in the world, a meritocracy without "unfair advantages."

This is the territory where Caster treads, and the waters she troubles: does she have an unfair advantage? Rivals claim that by virtue of her ostensible masculinity she has somehow gained an advantage that her presumably "more female" competitors cannot claim. "Just look at her," said Mariya Savinova of Russia. Elisa Cusma Piccione of Italy was even more aggressive: "I am not taking [Semenya] into consideration—for me she is not a woman. I am also sorry for the other competitors.... It is useless to compete with this and it is not fair."[10] In an age of performance enhancing drugs and vast inequities, a fixation on fairness is understandable, but it doesn't take long for the logic of these "fairness" arguments to fall apart.

In many ways sports are *all about* unfair biological advantages. That's what we love about athletic bodies. No one complains that Shaquille O'Neil is too big, that Floyd Mayweather has an unfair advantage because he's just naturally too quick, or that Brittney Griner should be barred from playing basketball because she was "born too tall." And if you want to talk "unfair advantages," what's really unfair and totally "unsporting" is that hundreds and hundreds of millions of kids are born into brutal poverty, and through no fault of their own do not have a fraction of the privilege afforded to many American or Euro kids.

---

10 Anna Kessal, "Rivals 'laughed and stared at' Caster Semenya, says Jenny Meadows," *The Guardian*, July 21st, 2010.

It's not even close to fair that some kids are fortunate enough to have unlimited family support, government backing, corporate sponsorships, swanky training facilities, well-paid coaches, sophisticated nutrition, and access to high-end equipment, while most other kids across the globe have nothing like those levels of support. Maybe we should be looking at centuries of racialization and constructing a solidly intersectional analysis of how and why particular folks feel so compelled and entitled to make sweeping judgements about bodies, and how often that means arbitrarily questioning "other" kinds of power and beauty.

But at another, perhaps simpler, level the notion that anyone can biologically or scientifically "prove" someone's gender or sex falls apart equally quickly. As Anne Fausto-Sterling wrote in *Sexing the Body*, and a legion of genetic and biological scientists have demonstrated since, there is absolutely no test that can "prove" someone's gender or sex. In a swarm of confusion and misrepresentation, Olympic officials have retreated to simple testosterone testing as a gender verification mechanism after years of using (and discarding) genital examination, hair patterns, chromosomal characteristics, individual genes, and other (mostly unexplained and irrational) factors.

The claim is that higher testosterone levels present an unfair advantage for women athletes, but even that notion is totally unproven and dubious at best: there is a total paucity of data about how testosterone reacts in women's bodies, or whether it would even aid athletic performance. And, from there, the more you poke at gender verification claims, the uglier it gets. Consider Maria Jose Martinez-Patiño, for example. She was a world-class Spanish hurdler who was found to be carrying a Y chromosome, but also has a complete androgen insensitivity (a syndrome called CAIS) which prevents her body from responding to testosterone and thus she developed as a woman. On the basis of these tests, she was disallowed from competing in the 1988 Summer Olympics despite being a medal contender. But her androgen insensitivity means that she cannot use testosterone at all, despite which she was able to perform at an elite level. So why exactly was she barred? Martinez-Patiño's case, like many other women with androgen insensitivity who have competed as Olympians, takes the legs out from the claim that testosterone is a necessary component of performance.

IT'S A GAME OF INCHES

What this all boils down to is the notion that it's time for us to accept that neither sex nor gender is a binary. We have to get over whatever fixations we might cling to about hard boundaries and recognize that there is a spectrum and that the vast range of human biological variation is inconsistent with two-sex ideology. So what to do? What should sports make of this? The simplest reflexive answer is an end to gender segregation in sports entirely. If it is functionally and scientifically impossible to describe definitively what constitutes male and female, then how can we have exclusively male and female sports events?

I'd say that's a great long-term goal: abandon sex segregation in sports and have open events across the board. But for right now, as a first step, that's a terrible idea. For a variety of reasons, maybe most importantly women and girls' access to structural and social support, even the most elite women athletes cannot compete with men in all but a very few sports. To dissolve women's sports in one fell swoop would crush female participation and visibility in a way that few of us could abide, and set back decades of progress in funding, anti-discrimination, and cultural attitudes toward women and sport.

It's very true that women are making significant gains and narrowing the gap between male and female performance at every level, but the gap is still very real. There are a few crossover athletes (like Danica Patrick, IndyCar and NASCAR driver), and a few sports where men and women currently compete equally (sailing, equestrian, horse racing) but there is no woman who could play in the NBA, NFL, NHL, or MLB right now.[11] But given equal access to resources, training, and coaching, alongside a vigorous undermining of sexist/misogynist social attitudes about women and their capabilities, it is highly possible to imagine a time when open competitions are viable. As folks like Katrina Karkazis and Rebecca Jordan-Young have suggested, rather than sex segregation, future sports events could have participants divided by size or weight, the way boxing and wrestling currently are. That's pretty good actually: that's a rendition of gender justice that compels me. But how to get from here to there?

To help me think this through, I went and visited Ann Travers at Simon Fraser University, who has written often and well about gender, sex, and sports. In a terrific essay titled "The Sports Nexus," Dr. Travers examines a number of possibilities for gender justice in sports beyond the ideology of two sexes, offering a roadmap of sorts. She suggests a range of legal/structural reforms that fall in the "hell yes, why are we not doing that already?" category. I've paraphrased most of them here:

---

11 Perhaps this seems a little totalizing, but it is not in any doubt. There have been episodic attempts like Manon Rheaume who played goal for Tampa Bay in a 1992 NHL preseason game, and Hayley Wickenheiser (2003, hockey), Nancy Lieberman (1986, basketball), and Katie Hnida (2002, football) all of whom have played very briefly in lower-echelon leagues, but there is no viable argument that a woman can play in a major sports league currently. It is commonly claimed that if any woman can legitimately help a team and win a position, she will be welcomed. I think that is essentially true, while acknowledging all the barriers to that happening and the shitshow that would ensue.

- Require all levels of sport to conform to occupational human rights standards relating to non-discriminatory practices with regard to development, recruitment, and promotion.

- Adopt a zero tolerance policy for racism, sexism, homophobia, and transphobia with consistent and meaningful consequences for violations.

- Consider and grant requests for government accreditation and support, including the granting and renewing of broadcast licenses only to sporting organizations that demonstrate compliance with said human rights requirements.

- Require amateur sport at all levels to invest equal resources into the recruitment, development, and support of male and female athletes.

I love these suggestions and they strike me as good-to-go, sans a lot of debate. Why are we providing public funds, broadcasting licences, university and amateur sport resources to any organization that doesn't adhere to human rights standards, including at the deeper recruitment and development levels? Sports leagues at every level can move really quickly when the spirit moves them and most leagues have already shifted significant distance in many ways, see for example the very slim tolerance for hateful on-ice/floor/field slurs.

Travers's bolder suggestion and one that really moved my yardsticks is to eliminate male-only sporting spaces at every level, but protect such spaces for women and girls (with trans-inclusive boundaries).[12] As she suggests, "adoption of this strategy would require sporting spaces and institutions

---

12 Meaning that transgender individuals would be included in these spaces should they wish to be, without having to "prove" that they are women.

that are currently all-male to abolish formal and informal mechanisms for single-sex recruitment, development, participation, leadership and employment." This kind of voluntary segregation would allow all people to compete with each other on a non-discriminatory basis, while still protecting women's sports, while they make up the gaps. We would never accept a sports space segregated on the basis of race, so why is gender any different?

This strategy would trigger a cascade of changes, from the peripheral (like voluntarily shared locker spaces and meeting rooms) to the fundamental (like social expectations of equal resources, support, and encouragement). The only question I had when thinking this through is the question of sex-testing: if we are going to continue to protect women's and girls' sports spaces, while understanding that many people do not conform to simple binaries, how do we know/decide who is a woman? Replacing men's spaces with open participation eliminates that issue, but who gets to be in women's leagues and competitions? Especially when we know that sex-testing is a specious idea? I was stuck on this point until talking with Travers. She argues that whoever says they're a woman should get to play in women's sports. Sure that'll cause a little debate and friction here and there, but really it will be minimal comparatively: "the damage of trying to perform sex-testing is far greater than what is inflicted on women's sports by allowing self-definition." My fear of some random male athlete claiming they are now a woman and demanding to be included is probably misplaced and unlikely to really happen, and in Travers's estimation, worth the risk. I agree.

THE FANS ARE ON THEIR FEET NOW

So, try that on for size.

Consider the suggestion that forms the main thrust of the book: that sports can be an irreplaceable arena for radical social change, and then consider sex and gender. I think it's true that people like Brian Burke, the Williams sisters, or Ben Cohen represent a living and breathing embodied practice that challenges deeply-entrenched and deeply-fucked notions about bodies and what they are for.

While I think it is certainly true that encountering bodies like Semenya's with generosity forces us all into new and better positions, the issue is only partially how other athletes will react. Commentators tend to focus on whether players will accept an LGBT teammate (with a special fixation on showers), but a much bigger question is how executives, coaches, media, and management will handle it. These folks tend to be older, more conservative, and less comfortable with everyday bodily interactions, as do many fans. But as Christina Kahrl told me, there are plenty of reasons to doubt narratives that anticipate bigotry.

I could scarcely be a bigger fan of Kahrl. Christina is a Chicago-based transgendered sports writer who transitioned in the middle of her career. As Chris, she was a respected writer for *Baseball Prospectus*. In 2003, she came out as a woman and since then has continued to work as a sportswriter and now works for ESPN.com, is a member of the Baseball Writers Association of America, and has also written for SportsIllustrated.com, the *New York Sun*, Salon.com, Slate, *Playboy*, the *Washington Blade*, and was an associate editor of *The ESPN Pro Football Encyclopedia*. Baseball is perhaps the most conservative of all sports: tradition-bound, densely populated by old white guys, resistant to change, grumpy—so it would make sense that Christina's experience would be challenging at best and deeply harrowing. Except it wasn't.

> The great thing about sports is that they keep defying people's expectations. When I came out in 2003 I had no expectations—I just said let's see how the world responds. I had no idea how it was going to go but many of

my parents, friends and co-workers were really outspoken in their support.

When I went back into the locker room nothing really changed. I went to work and didn't make a news event of it, I didn't announce it, I didn't make a big deal of it—and other people responded in kind. Aside from one person, all the athletes were fine. I have not encountered any active bigotry. It has really been a non-dramatic story. I had earned respect from previous years, but I also just wanted to do my job, just wanted to be a working stiff. Baseball has been very, very good to me.

People didn't freak out they just took it as a matter of course. I couldn't ask for a better experience, it could not have turned out better, when I think about it. When I interviewed with ESPN I was the one to bring it up. The BWAA is a mostly white, over 50, mostly male organization—but I was elected on the first ballot not as Chris, but as Christina—which tells you about people—about their everyday moral courage that is totally remarkable in some ways.

I think that when confronted with the real, instead of the abstract, people's response has been reliably admirable.

When many of my friends in the queer and trans communities find out I work in sports they say "Oh that must be horrible, people must be really mean to you," but no it's the reverse—it has been super easy, super fun—lots of the athletes are really cool with me and who I am. The expectation that athletes must bigoted is totally untrue—people and athletes are awesome. Sports are a vehicle for acceptance across difference.

My co-workers and colleagues have also been amazing. I am now visibly trans, but we are still just talking about baseball, like we always have. They have been reliably cool about being in public with a trans person talking about something we both care about—and that changes the dynamic when we share similar interests—I'm still just a sportswriter and I don't talk about baseball in any different way."

Obviously I fucking love this story, for all kinds of reasons. But as Christina points out, the real battles are not going to be fought in pro sports. The battlegrounds are going to be at colleges and in college sports, in K-12 sports, and with youth club teams. Those conversations and fights are going to be held in towns like Scranton or Tuscaloosa or Lodi or Moose Jaw. It's one thing is to hear about out athletes in the news, but when it happens in the schools, in gyms, right where people live, where states and school boards may not respond well, where kids who face bigotry don't get to play—that's where the real stories are going to play out. But if Christina's experience is any bellwether, maybe sports give us more reasons to hope than cringe.

These aren't answers per se. I don't think justice, gender or otherwise, is a "problem" we're ever going to "solve." It's something we're going to have to face, and live with, and think about, and work towards every day. Separating men and women, and discriminating against them accordingly on the field, floor, and ice resonates throughout our culture. What would happen if we took a chance and reversed field, if we worked from solidarity rather than nostalgicized prejudices? I can't imagine a better place to start than in the world of sports.

CHAPTER FOUR:

LEAVING THE FIELD UNDER OUR OWN POWER

VIOLENCE, COLLISIONS, AND EVERYDAY LIFE

In March of 1962, Emile Griffith killed Benny "The Kid" Paret in Madison Square Garden.

Griffith was a brilliant fighter—a Caribbean-born New Yorker, a six-time world champion, beloved for his speed, athleticism, and beauty. He won the welterweight championship for the first time in 1961, but relinquished it later that same year to the Cuban Paret who won the belt back in a split decision. The 1962 fight was the rubber match in a trilogy that was as ferocious as it was tight.

In the sixth round at MSG, Paret came within maybe twenty seconds of knocking Griffith out. Paret was landing cleanly and had Griffith in all kinds of trouble, trying hard to cover up along the ropes, and only the bell got him out of the round. In Griffith's corner, his trainer, the legendary Gil Clancy, went nuts on his fighter screaming at him: "When you go inside I want you to keep punching until Paret holds you or the referee breaks you! But you keep punching until he does that!" Griffith followed those instructions perfectly and in the twelfth round he was pummeling a helpless Paret in the corner. The fight had been fierce from beginning to end, and the referee had a very long look (mind-bogglingly, and kind of grotesquely) before stepping in. Paret sagged and sagged some more, but Griffith kept punching until Paret was draped like wet laundry over the ropes. He never regained consciousness and died ten days later.

The fight was televised nationally on ABC, causing the network to cancel its boxing coverage. No other network would broadcast boxing for a decade. It was exactly the kind of naked brutality that makes decent people cringe, turn away, and mumble about the decline of civilization, gladiatorial mentalities, and "what the fuck is wrong with all you people who cheered and all you animals who keep watching it on Youtube and all you rubber-necking a-holes who still cling to pathetic defenses of boxing." It is exactly the kind of argument being forwarded by those (and there are a lot of people) who want to ban fighting in hockey, football *in toto*, and combat sports in general. Try watching the Griffith-Paret fight and tell me you don't get all revulsively indignant and existential. Shit is nasty.

But wait. There's more to the story. The first important thing is what a good person Griffith was: Rest in Peace EG (July 23rd, 2013). He was a really decent, thoughtful, and caring man. In the dressing room after the fight, he began to get a sense of the injury he'd inflicted and kept repeating, "I hope he isn't hurt, pray to God—I say from my heart— he's all right." As the true extent of that damage came clear,

Griffith tried hard to visit the downed fighter in the hospital, and when denied ran through the streets of New York in horror. More than fifty years later, he was still tormented by the incident. I dare you, double dog dare you, to watch *Ring of Fire: The Emile Griffith Story*, and tell me he's not a great guy. And I dare you to watch the scene where Griffith finally meets Paret's son, and is forgiven, and not cry. It's a tremendously sweet, complicated story.

You see, Griffith was bisexual. He married a woman, but slept around omnivorously, and denied it to no one. It was an open secret in the boxing world, and to a lesser extent in the larger sporting world. Griffith was startlingly beautiful, had a gentle voice, dressed extravagantly, designed women's hats, traveled with a "personal assistant" widely understood to be a boyfriend, and while he was not "out," and that was not a matter to be trifled with in the '50s and '60s, he was definitely not closeted.

Paret knew this and taunted Griffith vigorously. At the weigh-in, Paret stood behind Griffith and called him a *maricon*. Griffith had to be held back: "I knew *maricon* meant faggot, and I wasn't nobody's faggot." Throughout the years since, Griffith consistently and respectfully reiterated his sorrow at Paret's death. But, he often added: "He called me a name.... So I did what I had to do. I got tired of people calling me faggot."[1]

In part, the story is compelling because it tidily reverses the tiresomely predictable narrative arc that gets the (usually helpless) gay character killed at the end of the story. It would be an unconscionable stretch to claim Paret's death as a justifiable moment of gay revenge,[2] and I don't really want to write something like "he deserved it." That's more

---

1   See *Ring of Fire*. Also Ron Ross, *Nine... Ten... and Out!: The Two Worlds of Emile Griffith* (DiBella Entertainment), 2008.

2   As Griffith said: "Anyone who said or wrote that I wanted to kill Paret was just vicious or stupid or both" (*Nine...*, p. 70).

than I can bite off right now. But the honest truth is that I keep thinking it. Paret's slurs and Griffith's power were not disconnected. Would Paret have died if he had chosen a less hurtful, less volatile insult? Paret knew what he was doing, meant to do it, and suffered the consequences.

In lots of ways, the story is useful here not just because it confounds easy thinking about violence, aggression, assertiveness, physicality, self-defense, and fairness, but also because it blurs a whole bunch of lines between violence in and around sports. When we're talking about violence and contact, we're talking about the collisions that happen between the lines, and the ancillary, but not unaffiliated craziness that is associated with sports: nutter fans, hooligans, fascistic coaches, brutal parents.

I'll argue that when Paret and Griffith were boxing, that was *not* violence. Paret's name calling, though, was violence, and Griffith crossed the line from consensual relationship to violence when he refused to stop punching even though Paret was clearly unconscious. Those distinctions cannot be disembedded from the larger social violence inflicted on gay men, in the 1960s at the time of the fight for sure, but hardly extinguished now. In a cruel twist, Griffith was very badly beaten and hospitalized in 1992 after leaving a Manhattan gay bar.

The key pivot in identifying violence is agreement. Not unlike various forms of sexual activity (say BDSM, for example), physical contact, collisions, and even bodily damage is not violence if consent is present. There are any number of physical, aggressive, damaging, risky, and painful activities that we all willingly and happily participate in that are not violence.

Sociological, psychological, and anthropological literature present a semantic jungle of attempts to schematize, categorize, and taxonomize various renditions of violence *vs.* aggression *vs.* assertiveness, most of which I am pretty skeptical about. I think it is wholly enough to name violence as: (attempted) damage done to another person as an act of non-consensual aggression. I think that's enough for here (let's talk about the instrumental uses of violence another time) and going all Žižekian and talking about symbolic linguistic or socio-economic systemic violence is not real germane and to a certain extent stylistic preening/contortionism. "Non-consensual damage" suffices.

I think there is significant danger in extending the definitions of violence any further and deriding or undermining the value of collisions and contact. The experience of physically running into other people, objects, and the natural world (sometimes powerfully) is vital and irreplaceable, not just as an expression of singularity, but for the possibility of community.

PLAYING SOME SMASH-MOUTH FOOTBALL

There are a couple of basic narratives about sports and collisions that are frequently voiced in bars, academic journals, living rooms, conferences, and locker rooms alike. The two arguments are kind of, but not entirely, contradictory. And neither is particularly useful in my estimation.

The first narrative claims that sports are a useful mechanism in an evolved society because they act as a pressure valve allowing men and, perhaps to a lesser extent, women a (barely) socially-acceptable outlet for their inherent barbaric and warring instincts. The suggestion is that men and boys are, at core, freaking nuts: driven half-mad by testosterone, rage, resentment, sexual repression, and a base animal drive to beat the crap out of each other and themselves. Sports are a proxy and/or replacement for actual war, and play an important role as a constrained pressure valve for the less-evolved among us.

I'm sure you've heard this shit more than once. At face value its sounds alright and makes for an easily flipped cliché, but as you might guess, I am not fond of this argument and find it both deeply condescending and full of the kinds of pseudo-scientific armchair-psychoanalytic and theoretically-dubious assumptions that dovetail nicely with both Randian economic logics and elitist pandering.

The wholly-unsupported assumption that human nature (whatever that might be) is inherently violent is the worst kind of essentializing. It is the kind of thinking that informs the demonizing of humanity as simultaneously brutal and helpless, and rationalizes crass ideological constructions of humanity's "natural" states, like the long-discredited "killer-ape" mythologies. I reject all of this, and concur with the Seville Statement on Violence that concluded (among other things) that: "It is scientifically incorrect to say that we have inherited a tendency to make war from our animal ancestors. It is scientifically incorrect to say that war or any other violent behaviour is genetically programmed into our human nature. It is scientifically incorrect to say that in the course of human evolution there has been a selection for aggressive behaviour more than for other kinds of behaviour. It is scientifically incorrect when people say that we have to be violent because of our brain. It is scientifically incorrect when people say that war is caused by 'instinct'."[3]

There is no beast inside us that needs to be released. Instead, we need to nurture the kinds of behaviors we admire and inhibit other kinds of behaviors. Those goals can be socialized in a myriad of ways, but rather than presume we need to drain the toxicity of violence contained within us, I'll suggest that we should look to sports as one site for nurturing the best in us. We do not need to describe ourselves as helpless victims of biology; I'd much rather have us writing our own scripts. As the Seville Statement put it:

---

3   See for example: http://www.ppu.org.uk/learn/texts/doc_seville.html.

"The brain is part of our body like our legs and hands. They can all be used for co-operation just as well as they can be used for violence. Since the brain is the physical basis of our intelligence, it enables us to think of what we want to do and what we ought to do. And since the brain has a great capacity for learning, it is possible for us to invent new ways of doing things."

Getting back to the question of narrative, let's look at the second argument, which is kind of the flip side of the first: sports don't relieve and mitigate the possibility of war and violence, they do the opposite. This argument suggests that sports normalize aggressive behavior and prepare young men for battle, real or imagined. The claim is that watching and/or playing sports jacks us up, inculcate us with the worst values, make us violent, xenophobic, and ready to start shooting here or there, wherever. As George Orwell proclaimed: "Serious sport has nothing to do with fair play. It is bound up with hatred, jealousy, boastfulness, disregard of all rules, and sadistic pleasure in witnessing violence: in other words, it is war without the shooting."[4]

I am equally antagonistic to claims like this. These two arguments are echoed often, sometimes implicitly, sometimes simultaneously. But which is it? Do sports make people more or less war-like and violent? There are other entwined and dubious arguments that often weave through these kinds of discussions: that watching sports makes us violent; that men will be men and boys will be boys; that people who like sports are biologically (or at least culturally) predisposed to aggression. There are lots of supercilious suppositions in there, and I think they are worth resisting. I have a good well of respect for Mr. Orwell, for all the

---

4   George Orwell, *The sporting spirit: Collected essays, journalism and letters of George Orwell, vol. 4* (London: Secker and Warburg, 1948/1968).

obvious literary and political reasons, but frankly, on this point, George can fuck right off.[5]

This proto-aristocratic sneering reeks of "civilized" paternalistic attitudes that strip people of their agency and social possibility, and avoid complex social and structural arguments. Do you ever hear people say this shit about chess, or debating, or similarly "intellectual" activities? What's more war-like than chess, both metaphorically and actually? The most aggressive and ready to pop off I have ever felt are playing checkers, ping pong, and tennis, maybe or maybe not in that order.

I think we need to talk about transformative possibility and the body, and particularly the idea of collisions. It's important to be aware of how people act in and around sports, and ways sports have been used in the service of nationalist/fascist tropes, colonialist ideologies, and male-supremacist fantasies. There is ugliness shooting through the sports world, from Raiders fans to soccer hooligans to sadistic coaches to misogynist bureaucrats, and they all need to be confronted, as do all of the other places where violence shows up, in all its forms.

But sports are *not* violence, and there are no contingent connections between physical games full of material collisions and violent attitudes/behaviors. To suggest that sports either quell or fan the flames of inherent male violence is to deny subjectivity, rationality, and possibility in ways that are decidedly reactionary. There are constellations of values and claims that need to be confronted and contested, but essentializing via low-grade psychological/anthropological musing is dubious at very best.

A much more useful approach is to contextualize sports within a historical, social, and cultural framework, acknowledge the deep meaning and value people derive from sports,

5   I thought about going all ironic here and threatening to beat Orwell's
    ass like a drum, but reconsidered due to general propriety.

and then seek ways that the sports world can become a force for good, both in and of itself, and instrumentally. I'd suggest that rather than revile and fear the physicality of sports, we ask what it is specifically about collisions that is so important, liberatory, and, well, *fun*.

To talk about collisions is to talk about risk. Without risk our lives become intolerable safety-first regimes: hermetically-sealed, sanitized dystopias where nothing ever happens. It'd be skiing only on the bunny slopes, no-touch hockey, never talking to strangers. We can certainly have reasonable discussions about how much is too much, what kinds of damage are worth it, and what risks we should be glamorizing. I'm all good with those discussions individually, familialy, and socially—surely we can disentangle them from retrograde narratives of masculinity and toughness—but it's more than that. We can start to make notions of thresholds and difference pivots for thinking about community and the possibilities of being with others.

A WHOLE NEW BALLGAME

Several years ago we were in Thessaloniki, Greece visiting old pals. After some prodding, my buddy Christos agreed to take me to a soccer game. It was pretty late Sunday night and pouring buckets of rain, but no worries. We jumped on his scooter and started hammering through town, but halfway there the bike stalled out. Without hesitation, Christos threw the thing to the side of the road (even though he really needed it for his job delivering pizza) and we broke into a half-trot for the last mile or so. I'd never seen him so jacked up.

I could feel Toumba Stadium before I saw it. There was the glow of the lights on the low-hanging clouds, the ocean-like roar of the crowd, but it was something else too. Something kind of low and rumbly with a *Lord-of-the-Rings*y epic quality. I noticed my man Christos had barely stopped talking in his busted-all-to-hell English, and now he was telling me that we didn't have tickets, but no worries, we'd just try to sneak in.

That sounded fine to me until we turned a corner and I saw the stadium. It was massive and new, but it was the cops that caught my attention. Due to long running and often brutal clashes between the home PAOK fans and supporters of Aris (the visiting squad), the apparently always-heavy police presence was now state-of-emergency grade. Every entrance was boxed in by 20'x20'x20' cubed cages of steel fencing topped with razor wire, and these bear pits were packed, shoulder-to-shoulder with fully thugged-out cops. I don't even know how anyone would get through, even if they had a ticket. Then surrounding that shitshow were concentric rings of more riot cops, all with huge shields, clubs, and visored helmets. I was all good for sneaking in, but it seemed outrageously unrealistic.

Christos and I, plus a pal of his who had joined us, circled the stadium, dodging rivers of hammered Greek boys—everyone geared up in black and white. There was not a square inch of yellow anywhere: it is illegal for Aris fans to gain entry to the stadium (due to the inevitable mayhem), and wearing anything like their yellow colors would be unnecessary provocation, guaranteeing a beatdown (at best). Finally, we came to Gate 4: a huge gaping maw in the side of the stadium. Direct access, no guards, no cops, no tickets required. Just a mix-mastering swirl of fans all tumbling around and in. Turns out there is a subsection of PAOK fans, the *Ultras*, who are so totally out of control that the relevant authorities have just given up on trying to handle them, opting for a containment strategy. Ergo: Gate 4.

Christos and I put on our motorcycle helmets and in phalanx formation, with his buddy (never did catch his name) at the wedge, charged in. It was maybe two or three minutes of jostling and negotiation, and then we found ourselves right there: great corner spot, sweet view, twenty-five, maybe thirty rows up, perfect really.

Total gong show: Bouncing, roiling, singing, chanting, drumming, bouncing mosh pit of a crowd. No seats (they'd long ago been ripped out and thrown onto the field). The section was caged off from the rest of the crowd with thick, fierce, razor-wire-topped fences. Surprising number of women in our section. Alcohol was flowing freely, passed around in flasks and jars. Every once in a while a person would get passed up or down. Flares and steamers shot overhead like anti-aircraft tracers. Fireworks and firecrackers crackled nonstop. Actually, there were flames everywhere, all the time. All along the bottom ring of the stadium huge banners were set on fire, and there were bonfires all through the crowd, and not just in our section, everywhere.[6] What were they lighting on fire? Some guys even climbed way up on top of the slick and super-modern digital scoreboard and started a fire. Plumes of smoke obscured sight lines in every direction, and the clouds of paper confetti didn't help. The rain didn't either. I asked Christos what some of the chants were saying. No delicate flower, he demurred and said they were just too foul to translate.

---

6   As I'm writing this it sounds absurd. Why was there so much fire everywhere? What the hell? Were there really flames everywhere, was it that crazy? You get ejected from any North American stadium if you so much as light a cigarette. How good would it be if you tore out a few seats and lit a bonfire? Would they just kill you right there, or wait until they dragged your ass down into the concourse?

I Youtubed the hell out of Toumba Stadium, PAOK, and Gate 4 and found an awesome series of videos—confirming that, yes, in fact, it is a madhouse, and if anything I was there on a somewhat restrained night. Have a look, especially at one of their Olympiakos matches. Unrelenting gong show.

The crowd started semi-hysterical and it went south from there. Every foul, every shot, every slightly promising run sent folks right to the edge of their sanity. When PAOK finally scored in the seventy-fourth minute, we collectively went well over the line. Among the notable responses to the goal was a short, tubby, hairy dude standing in front of me. He had lost his shirt, his Greek-style jheri curls were flat and mattered in the rain, as was his copious chest, back, and shoulder hair. His face was covered with snot, rain, frothy saliva/alcohol, and god knows what other liquids.

Christos was pounding my back hard enough that I almost had to take a knee. People were crashing into each other from all sides, hugging, leaping on each other, wailing. And this Hobbit-dude in front of me turns, screaming incomprehensibly, his whole body shaking with joy—he turns, grabs my head with both slippery hands, screeches something at a distance of about an inch and half, then proceeds to kiss me passionately, maybe seven or eight times, all over the mouth, eyes, lips, forehead, with his tongue well-engaged. I froze rigid. I couldn't move, or think, or breathe. The dude screamed once more, then turned back to the field and recommenced hucking shit from his pockets onto the field. I regrouped (semi-hysterically) fishing frantically for some dry piece of my shirt, then did everything possible to wipe my face and mouth off, including dousing my whole head from the first flask that came by in an admittedly futile nod to disinfection.

It was the greatest sports event I have ever attended. PAOK won 1-0. After the game Christos, buddy, and I wandered, dazed and exhausted (at least I was), out of the stadium and onto a street nearby where we stopped for a couple of beers and some food. The spill-over mayhem was dialed down a bit, but only slightly. There were people all over the road, a few cars overturned, some folks walking over them, lots of shirtless young men hollering, bottles and windows broken, a sort of low-key riot tableau. The three of us sat there and my companions, in some tenuous English, asked about Canada and sports. They had heard that for Canadians hockey approximated soccer in the popular consciousness, but was it true they wondered, was it *really* true, that the players were allowed to fight, like fight for real with *their bare fists*, on the ice? Can it be that this is sanctioned and the fans cheer and this happens often? Can it be that you too, Matt, are a hockey fan and watch this?

They were amazed and stunned that on-ice fighting was commonplace. They gaped and scoffed and Christos sputtered: "But that is barbarians! You are barbarians!"

WITH US OR AGAINST US

It's not just the wild passion/psychoses of fans at sporting events like the PAOK game that freak most of us out, it's the quasi or sometimes real fascist stench. Sometimes it's insinuated or latent, sometimes it's sitting there naked and unapologetic. You can see it an hour or two before game time at Toumba when the whole stadium claps and responds in rhythm to the beat of drums and you wonder how far off a Nazi salute is. You can see it at almost any major international event when chants of U-S-A! U-S-A! break out like ebola. You can see it in the consuming mania of college sports fans on their way to a football game, geared and liquored right up.

To many eyes, sports is affiliated with the worst nationalisms, parochialisms, and without being hyperbolic, very real fascist tendencies, usually implicit, sometimes ready to beat your punk-ass down. Seeing a soccer mob of hooligans up close is enough to terrify anyone into a loathing of sports. And sports have always been very pliable in extrapolating battles on the ice/field/court into metaphors for national pride and defense/aggression. As Travers and others have pointed out, the more closely a sport is tied to national identity, the greater the need to inscribe it with inherent masculinities that can be both defended and validated sometimes with violence/hostility, sometimes with misogyny, sometimes both: the Bondian "For England" rationalities.

Being a fan is about belonging to something bigger than you. It's a pack mentality,[7] it's Us *vs.* Them, it's having a crew to roll with, something to cheer for without restraint or reason. Those feelings of belonging and commonality and comradeship are vital, possibly even *requisite* to the human experience in a cold, infinite universe. They are the basis of community, of kinship, of neighborhood, and so much that we long for and hold dear. But those exact same sets of feelings are also the seedbeds of prejudice, hate, xenophobia, and fascism. There are all kinds of tipping points and they are rarely clear, except in hindsight.

The kinds of intense bonds that often emerge within and around teams and sports are perilously close to the totalizing logics of, for example, male supremacy or white supremacy. Sometimes what looks like a close-knit, loving team from the inside looks like a scary, insular gang from the out. Similarly, so much of the logic of community is built on an exclusivity, an In *vs.* Outness, and an ability to draw clean lines of demarcation between *Us* and *Them,* lines that have to be monitored, policed, and enforced.

Sports, especially those that carry iconic value actually and metaphorically—say, hockey in Canada, football in America, soccer many places—are especially susceptible to these narratives and often exhibit brutal kinds of intersectional insularities that both accentuate and ennoble the others. See, for example, the story of Lisa Olson, who in 1990 was a sports reporter for the *Boston Herald.*

As part of her job covering football, as with every other sports journalist, she was required to conduct post-game

---

7   Or, in my case, (Green Bay) Packers mentality. Sorry, couldn't stop myself.

interviews in the New England Patriots locker room. Some objected to her presence, a distaste that quickly turned to sexual harassment, with certain players fondling themselves and taking pains to parade naked in front of her, sneering comments, taunts, etc. She complained to the team. The then-owner of the team, Victor Kiam, called her a "classic bitch," and said, "I can't disagree with the players' actions" and claimed it was the *Herald's* fault: they were just "asking for trouble."[8]

Emboldened with official permission, the famously energetic Patriots fans turned against her. Her car tires were slashed, hate mail and death threats poured in, her apartment was broken into and vandalized, and far too few of her football beat reporter colleagues came to sufficient defense of her. Eventually the situation became so intense that her employer, News Corp, transferred her to Sydney, Australia where she worked for several papers covering rugby, Aussie rules football, and cricket. She won a settlement in 1991 from the team and in 1998 returned to the U.S. to work for the *New York Daily News* covering sports. She is member of the Baseball Writers Association of America and is a Hall of Fame voter, and continues to receive harassing phone calls and hate mail.

In a lot of ways this story will surprise approximately no one. Football players being sexist, vulgar, intimidating assholes? What a shocker. Football fans being psychotic, violent whackadoos? Almost unbelievable. But it's worth noting the confluence here of the Patriots (!), football, and misogyny: one legitimizing and giving permission to the other, leading to a violently unconscionable annexing of Olson's autonomy and body. In large part, it was the closeness and commonality of the team (and its fan base) that allowed for a

8   James Kunen, "Sportswriter Lisa Olson Calls the New England Patriots Out of Bounds for Sexual Harassment," *People Magazine*, October 15, 1990.

thug mindset, a group delusion, a mob-mentality just as much as it allowed for a loving community.

It's this fulcrum that is so problematic. When you're inside it, commonality, or "community" often feels fantastic: supportive, caring, loving, full of mutual aid and shared history. It's the narrative that pretty much all of us strive for via family, neighborhood, workplace, collectives, drinking buddies, friends, clan, team, club—and, for some, then writ large: country, ethnicity, gender, religion. But a striving for "Us" necessarily requires a "Them." Knowing who's *In* means making sure everyone knows who is *Out*, and then reinforcing those barriers by whatever means deemed necessary.

The degree to which we can make those boundaries permeable may be the key measure of whether our affiliations are plausibly ethical and alive. As soon as those edges become fixed and intolerant, that's the first and most critical ingredient for the ugly. Our families, teams, clubs, crews, and neighborhoods can be beautiful and life-affirming, fearful and bigoted, welcoming and hospitable, insular and parochial, big or small-minded, big or small-hearted—but they are all of those simultaneously, to greater or lesser extents. The yearning for a supposed hearth-and-home communalism that has been abandoned by modern society is not a particularly useful strategy, and tends to revert to naïve nostalgia, a romanticized mysticism that informs strains of conservative and progressive thinking alike.

The intensity of some sports affiliations makes them powerful and dangerous, sometimes akin to a racialized or nationalist fervor. Sports tend to fall short of the fundamentalisms of country and religion, but players and fans are susceptible to the same kinds of manias, especially when they become conflated with, and then transformed into larger narratives: those U-S-A, U-S-A Olympic chants turn into American exceptionalism and then predator drones mighty quick.

But are sports more likely than other affiliations to turn participants and spectators ugly, mindless, and/or violent? I think you'll guess that my answer is not necessarily: sports can incite a powerful kind of affinity, but just as that power is dangerous, it can be profoundly valuable. C'mon sports! Use your power for good, not evil! But I think getting us there requires a little theorizing about the nature of commonality.

"EVERYTHING I KNOW ABOUT MORALS AND THE OBLIGATIONS OF MEN, I OWE TO FOOTBALL"[9]

Part of the problem here is the movement from "I" to "we." Fundamentalist individualism views each of us as hyper-autonomous concretized monads, while fundamentalist collectivist renditions subsume those diacritic bodies into equally bounded units that cannot be impinged upon, and think and act with unified presence and purpose. It is taking the impermeable "I" and writing it large, into a faceless sameness: "We are Americans! I am Canadian!" And of course, "You are not!" It is ultimately the fantasy of the lone individual that informs the fantasy of the impervious, fixed "Us."

Our bodies are our own. We are singularities, but not really: our flesh is semi-permeable. There is a constant flow through our bodies of the natural world: air, water, food. The world around us *becomes us* at an astonishing rate, and our bodies regenerate constantly. We are shedding skin at a vicious clip: your whole outer skin layer falls off every 27–28 days. You shed about 600,000 particles of skin an hour—and grow it back just as fast. You grow a new stomach lining every three-to-four days. Your hair and nails are always growing, getting clipped, and/or falling off. We piss, shit, cry, drool, exhale, and sweat, and take in replacements,

---

9   Quote from Albert Camus.

all day every day. The physical world is constantly infiltrating us and us it.

And so are other people. I breathe in the air you exhale. I drink water that has been through countless people's systems. We share bacteria every day. We are one, not in the big hippie one-love sense, and not only in the butterfly-flaps-its-wings sense, but in the most everyday, quotidian, physiological sense. Our bodies are endlessly, physically permeable: in a very real sense your health is my health. To understand the singularity of bodies is to understand and nuance our own limits and thresholds, and the possibility of community—of solidarity with others—requires a visceral encounter with those thresholds. But not in a "*this is mine, that is yours*" sense: as Jean-Luc Nancy suggests, your existence is a necessary condition of my freedom.

Nancy massages notions of community, using singularity and plurality, not as polar antagonists, but as necessarily requiring each other. His ontological argument is that "the singular-plural constitutes the essence of Being," or put slightly differently, that "I" does not come before "we": there is no individual existence before or beyond co-existence.[10] The question, though, is how singular beings in plurality can avoid reducing the "we" to a singular identity: the position that spawns narratives like Serbs *v.* Croats, Hutus *vs.* Tutsis, Black *vs.* White, Us *vs.* Them. Nancy argues: "The community that becomes a single thing (body, mind, fatherland, Leader) ... necessarily loses the in of being-in-common. Or, it loses the *with* or the *together* that defines it. It yields its being-together to a being of togetherness. The

---

10 There's plenty of nuance and contention around Nancy's working of singularities/pluralities. Most of it is super wanky and academic, though there's some that I think are worth considering, but maybe not extensively here. Let's just say that I think Nancy opens up a really useful way to talk about reconsidering Us, Them, and the nature (culture?) of community.

truth of community, on the contrary, resides in the retreat of such a being."[11]

That retreat has to view commonality as simultaneously singular and plural, imprecise, malleable, shifting, porous, and contingent, just as the point at which my singularity ends and yours begins is not fixed. Those thresholds, too, are contingent and malleable. And the possibility of community, the being-with, depends on it. Fixing, or stilling, of a body's identity in place is a precondition for fixing the "Us" in place. The limits of my body, your body, and the natural world are (semi-)permeable: a condition that is often revealed to us in collisions. Dancing, lovemaking, sports, physical encounters with (touching) objects, and the natural world create the collisions that are the soil of everyday commonality, a radical plurality.

And pretty much all the time (and as age encroaches, *all* the fucking time), collisions bring with them the possibility of damage and pain. Pain and recovery, suffering and soreness are integral to plurality (even vicariously), and risk is part of the package. Sometimes it's just sore quads from biking or a blistered foot from walking too much; sometimes it's a flaring rotator cuff from swimming; sometimes it's the sprained ankle, the cut upside the lip, the tooth missing, the aching knees and abs; sometimes it's (a lot) worse.

Sometimes the pain is totally annoying, but mostly our damage is carried with pride, not just because we earned it, not just because it echoes pleasure, but because it marks our thresholds and the spacing[12] of community. It's common to gender pain relationships with narratives of manliness, or macho-posturing, but that misses the point. Stretch marks on a once-pregnant belly are not just lines on flesh. The scar on my temple is not just a dent on my dome.

---

11 Jean-Luc Nancy, "Preface," in *The Inoperative Community* (Minneapolis: University of Minnesota Press, 1991): p. xxxix.

12 The distances between you and me, between people and things.

In the residue of pain there is an inscription of vulner-ability, and possibly tenderness. There's a very particular feeling, a closeness that sports can engender. It's that feeling when that thug you have been practising a new jiu jitsu move with keeps checking if you're OK. This kid weighs two-sixty and has been repeatedly driving his elbow into my jaw, but at every break he looks kindly at me, rubs my back gently, and asks how I'm doing. We all know this feeling of closeness to someone after playing ball with them, banging hard in the paint for the last ninety minutes, the solidar-ity of the locker room, the way combatants collapse into each other's arms after the last bell, the mutual respect after training all day, sitting around the fire after surfing until dusk. And I'd extend that to the admiration one has for the mountain after you've hiked or skied it hard, or the respect you have for the ocean after being in it. We all know the sweetness of these feelings because they are so damn hard to come by elsewhere. It is in the pleasure of collision, and subsequent pain/damage, that we can catch glimpses of the porousness and contingency of singularity.

In collision, we sense (or in Nancian terms "touch") the thresholds of difference: not fixing identities, but confirm-ing them and their spacing—a spacing that is possible to play with, work with inside of a flexible, malleable differ-ence and a community that is bodily hospitable. It is a pos-sibility that is so often misapprehended, but carries with it not only the promise of neighborhood, but ecological pos-sibility.

It's kind of funny (a chagrined kind of funny) that I'm sitting here writing this chapter while watching a game at a bar, trying to understand my love of football and the irre-placeable value of bodily damage while nursing (yet another) concussion of my own. Picked it up about a week ago (can't remember when exactly)[13] playing basketball. Some kid got

---

13 That's a joke, c'mon. Really mom, I'm fine.

tired of me bullying him inside remorselessly and took a huge swipe, missed the ball, got my head instead, hitting the back of my skull so hard that my two contacts popped straight out before I went down. It was all good, no hard feelings or anything, but still a week later I have a slight tingling feeling in my hands, forehead, and teeth. I still feel a little …. there's a word I'm looking for here but can't think of it exactly.[14] Like Jim McMahon says, his concussions don't bug him too much, he gets to meet new people every day. Me too! They just happen to be my family.[15]

I get to joke about getting my melon dinged a little, because my cognitive capacity is hanging in there more or less. But that's nothing compared to these poor fucking football players who are getting concussions at truly alarming rates. The true extent of the neurological damage (let alone the mind-boggling damage done to the rest of their bodies) that is being incurred by football and hockey players (and boxers, MMA practitioners, rugby players, etc.) is becoming ever-clearer. The parade of NFL tragedy from Mike Webster to Dave Duerson to Junior Seau to Andre Waters to OJ Murdock to Ray Easterling to god-only-knows how many others and more to come is truly gross. I am not sure what exactly this carnage portends—maybe nothing, maybe the end of football as we know it if Malcolm Gladwell has his way—but the questions are all bound up with risk and personal agency in a late-capitalist era.

Virtually all players and a certain subset of fans want to argue that it is everyone's personal choice whether to play football or not because everyone knows the dangers: football is a physical game and people get hurt, sometimes maimed. This argument is not unlike those of mountain climbers, skydivers, free divers, speed freaks, and extreme sporters of all kinds: it's our choice, let us take whatever risks we

---

14 Seriously, I'm *fine*.
15 OK. I'll stop now.

deem acceptable. I am totally amenable to this reasoning in the case of say rock climbing, but football is another deal because there are other critical vectors here, mostly tied up around race, opportunity, capitalism, and spectacle.

I think football needs to aggressively regulate the damage inflicted on players. There is no question that a dangerous game is more exciting to watch, but my viewing pleasure is not commensurable with long-term participant brain damage. In the case of climbing, the risk is all individualized, but with football it is a social relationship: the willingness of players to take those risks is all bound up with my fandom which generates huge potential paydays. If there wasn't big-time money and fame involved, then I would say have at it, knock yourselves out (as it were!). But because football is fundamentally a social and cultural activity, we, as viewers, are implicated. To default to "it's a physical game and players know the risks" is a willful denial of responsibility, or: unethical.

These conversations cannot be just about individual choice; they are about the exigency of physical encounters to neighborhood, community, singularity and plurality—and the sporting world offers them up, time and again.

CHAPTER FIVE:

GETTING OUR GAME FACES ON

RACIALIZED CONVERSATIONS IN PLAY

Race and racialization have been running as a constant undercurrent throughout the first four chapters, but now is the time, hard on the heels of a chapter that pivots on touching, to focus on it a little more clearly. There is no way to talk about sports without talking about race for many, mostly pretty obvious reasons. And, in lots of good ways, there is no better place to think about race. Sports are where many of us encounter racialized difference most directly and viscerally, running into it skin on skin, always thinking about bodies, their capabilities, and their limitations.

It's sort of tempting to ask (self-consciously) opaque questions like: do sports abet racialized thinking? Do they undermine it? Well, the answers to both of these are obviously: yes and no, maybe, sometimes, depends, and possibly. But that's the territory I want to poke at. A better answer might be that sports are uncontrovertibly full of promise and potentiality, and a better question is: how might the sporting world legitimately combat racialization, white supremacy, prejudice, and privilege?

The sporting world has always insisted that athletic games present an ideal arena for ostensibly meritocratic performance: a place where all the bullshit claims for white hegemony are laid bare and stripped of validity—where people can compete fairly against each other straight up, and the weaknesses of racial prejudice can be both revealed and witnessed. In many respects this is true: there is a finality, an incontestability, a performative clarity that so often kicks racist presumptions right in the crotch. And many of these moments are iconic and stand as transcendent moments in modern culture.

Think of Joe Louis: the Brown Bomber. His fights were African-American celebrations[1] and affirmations of civil rights, but in beating Max Schmeling in 1938 (in less than three minutes!)—right in Yankee Stadium, in front of 70,000 fans, broadcast via radio to millions across the world, with live announcers in English, German, Spanish, and Portuguese—he was living proof of black power. Schmeling had beaten Louis two years previous and the Nazi regime trumpeted that victory far and wide, sending publicists everywhere with "their" fighter, claiming a black

---

1   As Langston Hughes wrote: "Each time Joe Louis won a fight in those depression years, even before he became champion, thousands of black Americans on relief or WPA, and poor, would throng out into the streets all across the land to march and cheer and yell and cry because of Joe's one-man triumphs. No one else in the United States has ever had such an effect on Negro emotions—or on mine. I marched and cheered and yelled and cried, too." Joseph McLaren, ed. *Autobiography: The Collected Works of Langston Hughes*, Vol. 14. (Columbia, Missouri: University of Missouri Press, 2003): p. 307.

man could never triumph over Aryan superiority. The fight was laden with nationalist implications, but as a moment of clarity it was a beautiful thing.[2]

It was a moment that echoed the four gold medals of Jesse Owens at the 1936 Berlin Olympics, when another black American athlete stomped all over Aryan-nation fantasies, right there in living flesh. Owens, himself, echoed Jim Thorpe (or *Wa-Tho-Huk*, "Bright Path") from the Sac and Fox native reservation in Oklahoma, who is generally acknowledged as the greatest athlete of the twentieth century (and maybe of all-time): winning the pentathlon and decathlon at the 1912 Olympics, and dominating professional football for years after, while playing pro basketball and baseball, and generally pulling off one ridiculous feat of athleticism after another,[3] despite constant and public incredulity that an Indian could be so spectacular.

Thorpe was doing his thing more or less simultaneously as Jack Johnson was becoming the first black heavyweight champion of the world in 1908 and then beating James Jeffries in 1910. Jeffries had retired as an undefeated champion without fighting Johnson, but was compelled to come back as the Great White Hope to challenge the black champ. Johnson's victory set off wild celebrations/race riots in fifty cities across twenty-five states. Johnson kept winning, while trash-talking and flouting every racial stricture he could, maybe most importantly, consorting with white women, and marrying three.

Each of these moments, and so many more, both famous and not, shine as points where claims of racial superiority

---

2   As is the story of Schmeling and Louis's lasting friendship, look it up—it's real sweet.

3   Like winning the 1912 Olympic pentathlon, competing in the high jump and long jump the same day, and doing it all after having his shoes stolen and wearing mismatched shoes that he found in a garbage bin.

and bigotry were defeated, unapologetically and unequivocally. Maybe the most reified of all is Jackie Robinson dropping the hammer on segregation in 1947. In breaking through discrimination in "America's pastime," and persevering through very public tribulations, harassment, and racist attitudes with particularly impressive style, Robinson's baseball successes (Rookie of the Year, MVP, Hall of Fame, etc.) became an everyday performance of civil rights. Day after day (and baseball plays so damn many games, it really was day after day), Robinson's bodily performance was a public antidote to bigotry.

And, all of that built a foundation for uncounted athletes thereafter, from Althea Gibson to Nancy Lopez to Jim Brown to Arthur Ashe to Wilma Rudolph to the Williams sisters to Roberto Clemente to Tommie Smith and John Carlos to Jeremy Lin to Park Ji-Sung: each breaking ground in their own ways, dragging every racialized attitude and callous claim out into the harsh light of reason. These folks, and millions of others, take every ugly slur—weak, stupid, lazy, inferior, cowardly, whatever—and dismember them in the glare of competition.

There has hardly been a site of greater integration, tolerance, generosity, and undermining of racial stereotypes than sports. So many of us have been able to learn intimately about one another by touching, watching, thinking about each other's bodies. Sports turn everyday playful acts of courage and strength and quick thinking and creativity and intelligence into performances of defiance, and in doing so give us something to talk about and rally round. And even the ugliness, all the sites of racialized thinking and acting—those, too, give us points of contact, something tangible with a common location of reference to comprehend.

Whether it's Rush Limbaugh slighting black quarterbacks, ESPN's Jeremy Lin "Chink in the Armor" headline, the guy you play ball with at the local community center who keeps making dubious racial jokes, Howard Cosell calling Alvin Garrett a "little monkey," or the billions of times people have challenged each other's implicit and overt racialized assumptions when playing with them: sports have given us something to talk about.

Or maybe not.

Maybe what sports have actually done, and continue to do, is calcify notions of athletes, especially black athletes. Maybe the relentless (and largely successful) push towards integration of athletics at every level has actually stabilized and reinforced racist notions about people's (particularly black people's) inherent capacities and predilections. And thus perhaps sports ironically confine both participants and spectators into a cycle of narrative presumptions about race and its performance.

Maybe it's the case that sports ironically and subtly concretize larger exclusions via specific inclusion: allowing African American and Hispanic athletes access to the highest levels of performance and success in the sporting world, while denying them anything like similar access and respect in other social arenas. As bell hooks says, writing about the movie *Hoop Dreams* in her essay "Neo-colonial Fantasies of Conquest": "In the United States, white folks wanting to 'enjoy' images of black folks on the screen is often in no way related to a desire to know real black people."[4] Perhaps the inclusion of African Americans in the sporting world does not undermine, but actually abets political and economic exclusion by allowing only very specific kinds of success and relationships, and then pointing to them as proof of equality and opportunity, cutting off more structural and substantive discussions.

And, maybe sports are a trap in another, symbiotic way: a sparkling blinging carrot that beckons young black men

4   bell hooks, *Reel to Real: Race, Sex and Class at the Movies* (New York: Routledge, 1996): p. 96.

especially in North America, and poor young men in every corner of the world, urging them to forget everything and reach for the (essentially) impossible ring of sporting fame and fortune. How can you blame kids sitting in a slum in Manila, a barrio in Caracas, a favela in Rio or a run-down house in Compton watching Manny Pacquiao, Miguel Cabrera, Ronaldo, or Serena Williams on the television and thinking that their best (and only) shot at *making it* is via their athleticism. Maybe sports resides with hiphop and crime in a false constellation of possibility: luring poor kids, urging them to forget their educations and intelligence, forget their more prosaic dreams, leaving 99% of them disappointed, broke, and often broken.

PLAYING WITH SWAGGER

One of the nostalgic tropes about American society is that social radicalism peaked in the late '60s/early '70s, and has been in slow decline ever since, giving ground, one defeat after another, to triumphalist neoliberalism. In some ways it's hard to deny that narrative, and sports are hardly immune. The days of activist athletes, of John Carlos and Tommie Smith, Billie Jean King, Bill Russell, Roberto Clemente, Curt Flood, Jim Brown, Kareem Abdul-Jabbar, and so many others who unapologetically tied their personal and professional struggles to larger social movements, have largely been replaced by a hyper-consumptive individualist ethic.

Most contemporary athletes are loathe to do anything that fucks with their precious "brand" or might compromise potential sponsorship deals. It's so banal, so freaking tiresome to listen to one more athlete hide behind some bland-ass charity, some tripe about "giving back" or "making a difference." You really have to struggle to find athletes today who are willing to say or do anything remotely politically progressive, let alone radical. We can talk the

Los Suns night, Etan Thomas, Mahmoud Abdul-Rauf, Cain Velasquez, Brendon Ayanbadejo, or Carlos Delgado for sure, we can talk about Magic's commitment to building businesses in black communities, but we need to dig pretty hard to find anything that moves the needle in a fundamental way.

I think it's fair to argue that a lot of the challenges to white, bureaucratized hegemony have become subtler, more nuanced and cultural: see Allen Iverson, Latrell Sprewell, or Michigan's Fab Five's issuing in a whole stylistic era of baggy shorts and unapologetic black swagger. Or Floyd Mayweather flaunting his "Money" handle. Or Charles Barkley, Warren Sapp, or Usain Bolt ostentatiously having fun, screwing around and mouthing off with impunity. Or every time a black athlete uses the word "slave"[5] talking about their contractual status. I think it is true that all these folks represent certain kinds of challenges to white supremacy, but I also think it's true that precious few twenty-first-century athletes are willing to risk much for larger social ideals. Like Carmelo Anthony said, "We're not allowed. We're not allowed. I mean everybody has their own opinion…you hear people talk here and there…but nobody don't really come out and say what they really want to say. That's just the society we live in. Athletes today are scared to make Muhammad Ali type statements."[6]

Is that it? Do sports today just reflect the world around them? Have times changed? They sure as hell have for athletes. And maybe that's it: maybe the money players make

5   It happens really a lot. A lot more than you might expect, which is totally interesting. See Gerald Early (*A Level Playing Field*) or William Rhoden (*The $40 Million Slaves*) for excellent discussions of this phenomenon.

6   Cited in David J. Leonard, "Not a Question of Courage: Anti-Black Racism and the Politics of the NBA Lockout," http://newblackman. blogspot.ca.

today is just too good, there is just too much for them to risk. Given the mind-bogglingly giant contracts drifting around and the steep salary trajectory that just keeps stratosphering, you can hardly blame athletes for playing things tight to the vest.

There are exponentially more journalists covering sports today than there were in the 1970s. I was one of them in the '90s, and the intensity is crazy-making. There is just so much sports coverage on so many platforms now that the competition for "news" is vicious. Every journalist (and pseudo-journalist, blogger, and joker with a camera) is rabidly hunting for any morsel to report and turn into a story. Any athlete that offers even a tepid opinion is immediately cycled and recycled into the Twitterverse, with every statement instantaneously dissected, analyzed, and critiqued. And, of course, anyone that strays even minutely from party-line orthodoxy gets crushed publicly, transgressions that threaten endorsement and possible contractual income.

Imagine yourself as a young athlete with the very real potential to earn tens (or even hundreds!) of millions of dollars sitting right there. Then understand that you can fuck that up, ruin the chance to support your family for generations, if you say one intemperate thing into that thicket of microphones wielded by pasty-faced, resentfully envious sportswriters. So why give them anything to work with? Professional sports leagues, their fans and critics do not want players speaking up about anything, least of all race or working conditions, and will punish those who do.

Then again, think of the global reach of Michael Jordan, Tiger Woods, Roger Federer, or David Beckham. Let alone the essential untouchableness of second-tier mega-stars like say, Rory McIlroy, LeBron James, Novak Djokavic, or Lionel Messi, just to randomly pick a few: really, these guys (and many others like them) could have a giant, positive social impact in innumerable ways, but to a person they choose not to.

The classic (and still unnerving) example is Michael Jordan's unwillingness to critique Nike's labor practises in even the most gentle of ways. "Be Like Mike" made Nike. Air Jordans built the Nike brand, legitimized it, and blew it up to an ungodly (or maybe godly) place in our culture: he has made his money, he is a worldwide icon, he has it all. MJ could and still can impact the lives of thousands of Nike factory workers with even a quiet, reasonable argument. But he didn't and doesn't.

Jordan made his feelings clear decades ago, though. In 1990, the former Mayor of Charlotte, Harvey Gantt, a black Democrat, was in a North Carolina Senate race against Jesse Helms, the notorious race-baiting, Confederate-flag-waving troglodyte. Helms was reviled internationally for his unapologetic tactics and stances, he was a racist icon. Gantt's campaign asked Jordan, a UNC alumnus and the most famous athlete in the world, for support. Jordan's response was: no thanks, "Republicans buy shoes too."

That's nasty, for sure, but MJ is just a little more callous than most. Everyone else is essentially saying the same thing. Think of the last time any superstar said anything remotely cool, anything you could reach for as plausibly political, or even a little risky. Then, think of Muhammad Ali and the impact he had, he has still. Think of his charisma, his fearlessness, his pride, his sharpness, the consistency of his overt integrity and willingness to say and do the right thing. And in lots of ways, his body tells the story of a political shift: from draft resistance, black power, and the Nation of Islam to mainstream adulation, Louis Vuitton, and Visa ads. In contradictory and complex ways he poses and answers the same questions I want to ask in this chapter, and then turns them back on themselves again.

A ROOSTER ONLY CROWS WHEN IT SEES THE LIGHT. PUT HIM IN THE DARK AND HE'LL NEVER CROW. I'VE SEEN THE LIGHT AND I'M CROWING.[7]

There really hasn't ever been anyone like Muhammad Ali. He has reinvented himself repeatedly, often compellingly. He has been lauded and vilified, honored and condemned, and remains resiliently complex and contradictory. But beyond his own machinations, a larger shift has occurred over the past couple of decades: an ongoing and relentless gentrification of his legacy.

From the very earliest public stirrings of his career, when he was still Cassius Clay, Ali affected an amazingly brash, vocal, and playful persona, rubbing almost everybody the wrong way with his audacity. While he was a patriotic Olympian, he was tolerated as just a youthful big mouth, but after he became champ—and, in short order, a politicized, name-changing, Elijah Muhammad-following, Malcolm X-associating, draft-resisting, strutting black man—he was almost universally loathed.

> I ain't got no quarrel with them Viet-Cong. No Viet-Cong ever called me nigger....
> No, I am not going 10,000 miles to help murder, kill, and burn other people to simply help continue the domination of white slavemasters over dark people the world over. This is the day and age when such evil injustice must come to an end.[8]

Jack Olsen wrote in *Sports Illustrated*: "The governor of Illinois found Clay 'disgusting,' and the governor of

---

7 David Remnick, *King of the World* (New York: Random House, 1999): p. 207.

8 Oft cited, see: "African American Involved in the Vietnam War," http://www.aavw.org/protest/homepage_ali.html.

Maine said Clay 'should be held in utter contempt by every patriotic American.' An American Legion post in Miami asked people to 'join in condemnation of this unpatriotic, loudmouthed, bombastic individual.' The *Chicago Tribune* waged a choleric campaign against holding the next Clay fight in Chicago.... The noise became a din, the drumbeats of a holy war. TV and radio commentators, little old ladies … bookmakers, and parish priests, armchair strategists at the Pentagon and politicians all over the place joined in a crescendo of get-Cassius clamor."[9]

In the early '70s, though, as larger political opinion shifted and suspicion of the Vietnam War grew, Ali emerged from the national doghouse and resumed his fighting career to a degree of grudging admiration and a (somewhat) muted chorus of detractors. As his boxing bravery propelled his career from courageous champion to patently damaged goods, dominant opinion turned once again, completing the cycle and becoming respectfully sympathetic and pitying.

Now the name and legacy of Ali has undergone yet another transformation: he elicits a strange kind of reification, a reverence evoked by Martin Luther King, the Kennedys, Mother Teresa, Gandhi, or Nelson Mandela, a larger-than-life implication of righteousness. It is the kind of ambiguous, malleable reification to which so many cling so tightly: a fractured yet reinventable legacy loosely invoking tolerance and progress, good-naturedness and good thinking.

There is little question that the general public/media have energetically leapt on the Ali bandwagon in part because the man has been rendered safe with age, disease, and mellowing. No longer the cocky force of nature, he is now humbled, personally and physically, making him safe and accessible. Observers of all stripes are able to get their dose of "edginess" by voyeuristically genuflecting at the Ali shrine, while staying comfortably insulated from

9   Jack Olsen, "A Case of Conscience," *Sports Illustrated*, April 11· 1966.

the political implications that the association might once have implied. With his viscerally historical moment largely passed, Ali can be recast as an archetypical success story validating the American egalitarian narrative: an assimilationist prototype, a weapon turned on itself.

Maybe even more than that, dominant media is now happy to glamorize black power and soul brothers/sisters, now that the Nation of Islam, the Panthers, and Black Nationalism are mostly muted and the once very real and prescient threat of black revolt has been rendered largely latent. It's a process of cultural gentrification that radicals everywhere are well acquainted with: once the political power of social movements is blunted, hyper-capitalist cultural forces hawk over the remnants with consumer satisfaction. That shit can move product.

This is not to suggest that Ali is not worthy of study or adulation: he absolutely is. There is no question that his legacy of transcendent (and transgressive) personality, vibrancy, attitude, politics, kindness, generosity, and beauty is needed now more than ever. The question is how to remember him and why. His legacy should cock people's triggers, not reduce them to nostalgic two-dimensionality.

The cultural gentrification of Ali easily follows in the footsteps of the legacies of Martin Luther King, Che Guevara and so many others. Ali can now be spoken of and commodified in ways never before possible. Insulated middle-class fans and advertisers can have their cake and eat it too: add funk and flavor to their postures without ever having to risk anything real.

This is the dangerous capacity of late capitalism: to transform even the most powerful people and social movements into cultural artefacts. Radical thought has always been susceptible to its own reduction to a lifestyle ethic, an attitude, or a pose, stripped of its political implications. There is nothing so satisfying as an edgy, styling persona to gentrify.

"I AM AMERICA. I AM THE PART YOU WON'T RECOGNIZE, BUT GET USED TO ME. BLACK, CONFIDENT, COCKY. MY NAME, NOT YOURS. MY RELIGION, NOT YOURS. MY GOALS, MY OWN. GET USED TO ME."[10]

Any consideration of Ali's trajectory has to fundamentally acknowledge his liberty and his politics, but also the tremendous punishment he absorbed in defense of his title: physical, intellectual, financial, and emotional. In standing up and refusing to hide, he made himself a target, and that is at the core of why he should be celebrated: not because he came back to the pack, humbled and stripped of the threat he once possessed. We should celebrate him *because* he stepped out of line, *because* he was willing to take shots and laugh, *because* he was like no other: because he was so dangerous.

The contemporary narrative strips away the complexity, while reconstructing his story as a palatable rags-riches-rags, feel-good special. I think much of the fascination with Ali revolves around his fall, and the implications of his tangible mortality and the inferred failure of his challenge. It's a smug paternalism that minimizes the content and radicality of his intentions, reverting to an interpretive arc that has little to do with the stew of racial, sexual, and cultural politics that Ali stirred so easily. Over and over we fixate on how physically damaged Ali is, how muted and devout his presence is now, and how he is just one of us, human. As Gerald Early says, "Now the public, because of Ali's illness, wants to drown him in a bathos of sainthood and atone for its guilt."[11]

By laminating and depoliticizing the myth of Ali, by idolizing him, and rendering him artefactual, he is reduced

---

10 Vorris L. Nunley, *Keepin' it Hushed: The Barbershop and African American Hush Harbor Rhetoric* (Detroit: Wayne State University Press, 2011): p. 5.

11 Gerald Early, *The Muhammad Ali Reader* (New York: Harper Collins, 1998).

and so are the transformative possibilities of his legacy. Ali is so much more than that though, and radicals have to pay attention to the idea of heroes and how their memory can honor and inspire the values that we ostensibly hold dear. How can we turn the tables once again, so that celebrating Ali illuminates, rather than conceals, our most intense contemporary social contradictions?

We have to be willing to read Ali as he was and is: defiant, radical, ironic, complex, devout, contradictory, transformative, confusing, dangerous, and all the rest—and we have to resist placing him within the easy trajectories that are so cheap and familiar. Considering Ali has to do more than reciting funky-ass poetry or feigning rope-a-dope, it has to be about throwing some punches too.

Let's get back to the question I set out at the start of this chapter: how can the sporting world legitimately combat racialized domination? I think the challenges here are similar, but just as racism shifts, morphs, entrenches and re-entrenches itself, resistance and antiracist thinking has equally to shift and evolve. The ease with which even the most powerful among us can be commodified speaks not just to the adaptability of late-capitalism, but the need for a sporting epistemology that confronts white supremacy as an everyday politics.

International high-performance sports make up a highly diversified landscape, one that's heavily populated with millionaire and multi-millionaire black, African, Latina/o, Caribbean, Asian, and Islander athletes. At virtually every professional and amateur level, efforts for integration have been highly successful (more so than virtually any other social sector), but to what extent does that damage and/or calcify racialized thinking in society in general? Racism has hardly been extinguished within sports, but can the experience of difference within the sporting world inform the rest of our lives?

PLAYING WITH A SENSE OF URGENCY

I wanted to think about this with an old friend, Richard "Bear" Peter, so I got him to take me balling. Rich is a great guy, a straight-up star. He is a five-time (!) Paralympian, three-time gold-medalist (!) playing for the Canadian national wheelchair basketball team. He and I grew up in the same rural part of the West Coast and have been pals for a couple of decades now. He is indigenous, from the Cowichan reserve on Vancouver Island, and was paralyzed from his T-10 spinal vertebrae down after falling under the school bus when he was four years old.

Richard was the only native athlete in the 2012 Paralympics, one of a very few in the 2012 Olympics total, and the more I talk with him the easier it is for me to grasp what indigenous athletes face. It's not just the everyday racism and doubt, it's self-doubt and cultural biases, it's the entrenched structural and social barriers that both reflect and construct larger white-supremacist narratives. But there's an athletic pivot there that I think gives us a chance to bodily think about resistance.

I had all kinds of ideas about my latent wheelchair basketball skills. I can play, stand-up that is. I've played hard since I was a kid, like to think I can hang with most anyone on most any court. That's full of middle-aged delusion (of course), but just let me have it for now. Point being, I was pretty sure I was going to rock at wheelchair basketball.

Years ago when he lived just down the street from us in Vancouver, Richard was a regular attendee at our big Sunday night dinners. Most nights after the meal a pack of us would spill out onto the street for semi-drunken Nerf football games in the dark. The first time he joined us, I matched up against him as a receiver/defensive back pair. I immediately started talking all kinds of trash to him about how I was going to catch one pass after another over him, how the hell was he going to defend me? I was just going to go deep, call for a lob pass and catch a high ball—dude you can't get out of your chair, I'm going to run rampant here, and so on.[12] Rich just looked at me and said nothing.

So at the first snap I did said thing: went deep and hollered for a bomb. Lakewood Drive is a bit of a hill so I sprinted easily maybe twenty-five yards looking for a quick TD. Richard was five yards behind and as I turned looking for the ball, he gunned right at me, full-velocity, speeding downhill, aiming his metal-framed chair right for my legs. The consequences were dire and immediately evident: with cars parked on either side of the street, I was in serious trouble. Equally clear was that after all my shit-talk, Rich was likely not stopping. I abandoned my route and dove out of the way, pass incomplete. Getting up and running back to the huddle, I tried to keep talking junk. Rich still didn't say much, just gently smirked at me.[13]

---

12 Stay classy, Hern.

13 At this point, as I was revising the book, my editor, Kate, who is straight-up brilliantly sharp, and avowedly not a sports person, made a note that said: "Do you really want to go here? I read this, and I think 'This guy is a total jackwad. Shut up.' Now, obviously, I know that this is not true about you, but random readers do not, and for people who maybe aren't as comfortable with this as you are (and your friend is) it seems really weird." First, that's funny as hell. Totally made me laugh. I told the story at the dinner table, and now my sixteen-year-old periodically tells me not to be a jackwad. Second, I agree that it does sound like I am a total asshole (and that is true to a certain extent), but it is also true that trash-talking and teasing play a really important part of sports culture that should not be laminated. Gentle junk-talking is a way to get past polite barriers, to say the monstrous in the spirit of friendship, to have fun, to try and touch and be touched, closer to the heart. It is a delicate balance for sure, because what sounds like harmless teasing to one may be mean-spirited and hurtful to another. It is an art, for sure, and I am not always the most artful. But it is a hugely valuable art that plays

That incident was still in my mind twenty years later as he gave me his good chair to play in, but I have remained cocky enough to think I'd pick it up pretty quickly. Right away I noticed that the angles are all different and my shot trajectories needed to be radically recalibrated. There are all the nuances of the chair: speed, changing direction, turns, feints, balance. Then figuring out how to dribble (three pushes without is a travel), find shooting lanes, position the chair vis-à-vis defenders' chairs, pick the ball up using a wheel, change hands to protect the pill: all of it is basketball as you know it, but confounding.

After about forty minutes of practice, I bugged Rich to play a little one-on-one with me. He was a bit reluctant, and in about three minutes I understood why. I couldn't really compete in any meaningful way—every time I tried to make a move his chair was in my way and I had no conceptual framework for figuring out how to get around him, he just blocked everything. On defense, he seamlessly changed direction and left me reaching and flailing randomly. It was no game at all, like playing against a six-year-old or something. I loved the whole thing but holy shit, it's tough. I was tired in a weird way, my core all fatigued, my fingers bleeding, and ready to regroup on foot.

Afterwards, we went out for some burgers and talked about his career. We talked lots about all the victories, the crazy number of countries he's been to, the four years he has spent playing

---

an important role in many cultures and circumstances. There is a lot of academic (primarily anthropological and psychological) literature on this topic, but Jane Austen put it well: "For what do we live, but to make sport for our neighbors, and laugh at them in our turn?" In this case, the fact of Richard's disability might be socially awkward and confusing; instead, Bear and I try to make it speakable and acknowledged—it is a central fact of his life, and there is no ignoring it, so why not make it (with love) worthy of humor and conviviality, worthy of respect?

pro ball in Europe, but I wanted to ask about what it was like being a native athlete. I had never really asked him much about it before, and I was surprised at how quickly and definitively he spoke about the racism he has encountered, the slights, the lacks of understanding. Rich is so placid, so chill, so easy-going that hearing him describe his encounters with racism as "all the time, everywhere" unsettled me a little.

I didn't think of it (of course I didn't) but people consistently assume that a native guy is in a wheelchair because of a drunken incident, driving or something. He's heard often that he isn't a "real Indian" because he doesn't speak "native" enough and has gone to school. Teammates have no idea what reservation life is like. Coaches have no comprehension of or tolerance for indigenous learning styles. Opponents drop racialized insults. So many family members at home going wanting and asking for money. People see the chair, then realize he's native, and from there it's on him to fight the incipient paternalism and prejudice—a fight that at several points he has just wanted to leave behind and move back home.

It's a story I have heard and read in several incarnations: brilliant young indigenous athletes keep running into so much bullshit and so many coaches/teammates who cannot cope with native epistemologies that they give up on their playing dreams, and let the gravitational pull of supportive, safe home communities bring them back. There's also something in there about the collectivist ethos of many indigenous worldviews that can discourage the individualist striving and arrogance that is openly presumed necessary to succeed in sports.

Richard has scrapped and hung tough through all that, been named Canada's Aboriginal Male Athlete of the Year and Canadian Wheelchair Male Athlete of the Year, won a giant pile of medals and awards, and now is in BC's Sports Hall of Fame. He is a distinguished, accomplished, and lauded (recently retired) athlete, and still he has got to be careful to watch what he says and who he says it to.

I asked him how he felt about wearing "Canada" across his chest, repping the country in international venues and wearing his national team gear—when that same Canada is responsible for the genocide of indigenous nations across the continent, and for forcing his Cowichan people onto reservations that are wracked with poverty, on a fraction of their rightful lands. He was straight up and it rang so true:

> Yeah, it's ironic and tough to swallow. I definitely have to bite my tongue sometimes. But the national team has paid my way for more than twenty years and I've got to do my part to give back. I'd really like to be more political, but I don't want to be a jerk and argue all the time. And now I've got to figure out what kind of work I want to do, and these gold medals are what I have worked so hard for. That's why you want to interview me. That's why people invite me to talk to schools. That's why I have a chance to work with native kids. That's why the Cowichan nation is so proud of me.

Listening to him made so much sense, in no small part because he's an old pal who I care about a lot, but also because I got so clearly the precarious position he is in, how much he has invested, how much he has at stake, and how much he has had to fight through. As he talked, it struck me how fucked it is to blame young indigenous, black, Latino, or Caribbean athletes for not speaking out more. Sure we've got to honor and defend every player who takes a stand, whether it's Adonal Foyle or Toni Smith or someone in the neighborhood, but to *expect* it of athletes is to underestimate the repercussive effects of racism and classism.

Sure, the highest-paid athletes make ridiculous money, but that's only at the very thinnest of the top echelons. The vast majority of pro and high-performance athletes make considerably less, and many make surprising little. Their careers are totally fragile (they are always just one hamstring or rotator cuff tear or emotional dip or consuming family issue away from it all falling apart) and typically very, very short. Despite the perceived strength of player unions in some sports (see: NHLPA after yet another work stoppage), in reality the overwhelming bulk of athletes, say Olympic athletes, have very little representation, limited post-playing options, and hardly any worker autonomy. Even at the very top end (and increasingly so the further down you go), the control and exploitation of athletes is a given: "The fact is that professional players offer their labor power to the factories of spectacle in exchange for a wage."[14]

So, sure, Jordan should say something. Sure he's an asshole, but why hold up Carmelo or Richard or whoever as "not doing enough" to speak up for racial justice? C'mon. Really, we should be going hard at owners, media, intellectuals, and fans for all the racial bullshit we let pass without a peep.

Consider for example the Washington Redskins. *Really?* The fucking *Redskins?*

Let me channel Ward Churchill[15] for a minute here, and let's imagine I was going to start a new sports franchise and was hunting round for a name. Let's say I wanted put one in NYC and, to "honor" the African-American heritage of the city, decided to name the team the New

---

14 Eduardo Galeano, *Soccer in Sun and Shadow* (London: Verso, 2003): p. 204.

15 If you haven't read Ward's "Let's Spread the Fun Around," do hit it. It's totally worth your time and is widely available online, as well as in The Purple Thistle Centre's *Stay Solid: A Radical Handbook for Youth* (Oakland: AK Press, 2013).

York Negros. Or, maybe if I was going to put the team in Baltimore, the B'more Blacks. Those would go over well I'm sure. How about the San Antonio Spics? That'd be appropriate given the large Mexican community in Texas. Or the Los Angeles Asians? Maybe the San Francisco Slopes is catchier.

Churchill keeps extending the fun to every racialized and discriminated-against segment of the population, and as he goes on it becomes crazier and crazier, the Kansas City Kikes, the Pittsburgh Polaks, Fresno Fags, Richmond Retards, etc. It's a brilliant trope and so awful that I can barely repeat it here. But it hits hard: just the idea, even the joke of naming a team, say, the Brooklyn Blackskins is so absurd and racist that no one would even consider it, even for a moment. But every major newspaper, every sports columnist, every ESPN highlight reel happily talks about the Washington Redskins without batting an eye.

That's hardly all of it. Think of the Atlanta Braves and their Tomahawk Chop, with 60,000 fans all chopping the air and chanting together. Or the Kansas City Chiefs. Or the Chicago Blackhawks. Or the Cleveland Indians and their crazily offensive Chief Wahoo mascot plastered on every imaginable piece of team paraphernalia, including their playing hats. Or the scores of universities and high schools with names like the Illini, Seminoles, Utes, and Fighting Sioux. Think about all the absurd mascots, celebrations, and rituals that these teams bank on. How would it go over if instead of a "chief" riding around the field waving an axe after a touchdown, a few performers overdressed like loin-clothed cannibals came out with bones through their noses, and danced around a stew pot waving spears? How about instead of the Tomahawk Chop and "war chants," the stadium passed out watermelon and fried chicken? That idea is so grotesque, it's unthinkable. But when it's native people, it is supposed to be in good fun and "honoring."

Is it any wonder why indigenous athletes often feel like they are entering sports arenas misunderstood, dispossessed, and prepared for degrading comments/opinions? There have been some significant movements at the high school and collegiate level, with more than 600 schools dropping their names since the 1970s, and the state of Oregon has banned all high schools from using native nicknames and mascots. But there's no movement at the pro level.

Defenders of the Redskins, Indians, et al. argue that the imagery is iconic to their franchises, that no harm is really meant, and it would mean so much trouble, such a huge expense, and such a tremendous upheaval of tradition and loyalty and memory, that it's just not worth the trouble. Aside from general obnoxiousness, this argument rings blatantly false in an era when teams are constantly changing their uniforms to access new revenue streams, but is especially hurtful in Washington where, in 1995, the basketball team changed its name from the Bullets to the Wizards after one (more) spate of DC-area gun violence.

Churchill argues, and I concur, that in the context of ongoing native genocide and displacement, the incessant propagandistic attempt to dehumanize indigenous people "in American popular culture is not "cute" or "amusing," or just "good, clean fun … it causes real pain and real suffering to real people. Know that it threatens our very survival."[16] It is in this context that I now recognize what a stupid question it was for me to ask Richard. Why do we (in this case, me) ask native athletes to speak out, when after 400 years of colonialism they remain in a precariously vulnerable position? Why is that on them, and not on those who still benefit from a legacy of land theft (again, like me)?

I think the same thing about young black athletes. I just took a break from writing to watch RGIII[17] highlights: the

---

16 Ibid.

17 Robert Griffin, III—the electrifying young Washington quarterback.

kid is unbelievable. Griffin is widely acknowledged as the most exciting player in the NFL, and took the league by storm as a rookie, with one sensational play after another. He is a delight to watch, but is ostentatiously pious on the field. After seemingly every play, he crosses himself performatively, points to the sky after touchdowns, and constantly talks about his religious beliefs. He also seems like a nice-enough guy: composed, thoughtful, sharp, and sweet. He also plays for Washington, and I wonder, with the city in the palm of his hand, what would happen if when he talked about Jesus and prayer and stuff, he also talked about the Redskins logo and how deeply offensive it is? It would be freaking awesome. But I cannot, and should not, expect that of him in the context of ongoing and pervasive racism, African-American discrimination, poverty, and precarity. If RGIII wants to leverage his position to say something positive to contribute to wider social goals, I will sing his praises. Until then, I will enjoy his football.

But I will also continue to speak (very) ill of Daniel Snyder,[18] and every Washington football fan who continues to wear the bullshit Redskins logo on any shirt, hat, or paraphernalia. I will deride any sportswriter, columnist, talk-show host, or fan who continues to deny the overt racism of the team name and fails to do something, anything about it.[19]

---

18 The almost comically Napoleanic and contemptible owner of the Washington football club.

19 As I have been writing this chapter there has been another push to get the team to reconsider the name, including ten members of Congress writing a letter to Snyder and the NFL that included this line: "Native Americans throughout the country consider the 'R-word' a racial, derogatory slur akin to the 'N-word' among African Americans or the 'W-word' among Latinos." NFL commissioner Roger Goodell rebuffed the effort calling the name a "unifying force that stands for strength, courage, pride and respect," while Snyder was even clearer,

SHOOTING THE LIGHTS OUT

This gets us back to asking why we don't take sports more seriously. That seems crazy in a land where, at one level, sports are taken more seriously than almost anything, but, at another level, are disregarded and condescended to. I think that if we genuinely took sports seriously, as something other than a trivial pastime, surely we wouldn't be able to ignore the endemic racialization in these team names.

Returning to my core argument here, I think that if we paid sports due respect, if we acknowledged just how much sports matter, we might not only be able to acknowledge sports as a unique and irreplaceable site for undermining racialized thinking, but for wider social transformation as well. In many ways, there is nowhere better than sports to talk about racialization—the sporting world has been able to realize a significant degree of sophisticated resistance to white supremacy. Think about the nuanced popular discussions around black quarterbacks and black leadership. Think about the Rooney Rule—an NFL-wide regulation that requires all teams to interview minority candidates for all head coaching and senior front-office openings—a rule that actually has teeth and fines teams if they try to circumvent it. This is just one very specific thread: think about how many times you have encountered contoured and thoughtful discussions about race with and from people you never would have expected.

It is in part because we don't take sports seriously enough, because we ignore them, because we allow the sports world to be so gross so often, because we let retrograde Chomsky-esque[20] takes on sports stand—that it is so hard to make

---

saying "We'll never change the name. It's that simple. NEVER—you can use caps."

20 I should note that, on the whole, I have nothing but respect for Chomsky. He has done as much as anyone over the past fifty years to articulate a principled and powerful opposition to American

that jump, to move sports from a condescended-to, isolated site for internal integration and racial progress to a larger dismantling of white supremacy. I would say that it is exactly those all-too-common paternalistic attitudes that calcify sports, and athletes, as a racialized spectacle, and prevent them from becoming a larger force for good. If we were open to understanding how much sports can and do matter, then we might have an embodied epistemological basis for undermining racialized thinking, for acknowledging all athletes, famous or not, as making legitimate, important social and cultural contributions, worthy of our attention and respect.

imperialism and generalized capitalist aggression/domination. Yet I think it's important to take him on here, in part because I think he is straight up wrong on this, but also because he articulates unambiguously what I think is a commonly-held stance.

CHAPTER SIX:

BLOWING THE GAME WIDE OPEN

CLASS, CREATIVITY, BELONGING, AND SOLIDARITY

It is pretty common to claim that the endemic disrespect of sports is primarily a class thing. And I'd say that's on the mark, at least in part. The sneering disdain that (some) privileged folks have for the lower classes who engage in corporeal games and base, animal expressions of play, is to be expected. We are all used to the civilized tropes that elevate mind (and/or soul) over body, and deride the intelligence and moral capacities of those who play and/or watch. But I am making a case for an intersectional analysis here: that a generalized disrespect for sports, athletes, physicality, and even materiality is not *just* a class thing, it's also bound up with race, gender, sexuality, and lots else—creating a clusterfuck of bodily loathing, fear, guilt, shame, distrust, and misapprehension.

Because this disrespect of bodies and materiality is so intersectionally experienced, and shows up in so many guises and costumes, disassembling it has to come both asymmetrically and asystematically, but also consistently. And for sure, a heavy load of that responsibility falls on sports fans and athletes. So many people spent major portions of their childhoods trying to be a part of the community that sports provide, only to find themselves ostracized, belittled, and/or ignored: so, of course, bitterness and hostility can stick around, right into adulthood. And rightly so. Sports constitute, in so many senses, a self-marginalizing and exclusionary system that reinforces its own (perceived) irrelevance by clinging to regressive politics and cultural ignorances. All of us who love sports have to own this and make our games worthy of the respect of our neighbors.

At the same I think it is incumbent on those of every political stripe and aesthetic persuasion to disassemble their own, often implicit or unconscious disrespect for sports. I'm most interested here in challenging radicals, leftists, and progressives of all kinds to look closely at whatever condescension for the sporting world they carry (often even if they are sports fans) and see instead the transformational potentialities.

> The scorn of many conservative intellectuals comes from the belief that soccer-worship is exactly the religion people deserve. Possessed by soccer, the proles think with their feet, which is the only way they can think, and through such primitive ecstasy fulfill their dreams. The animal instinct overtakes human reason, ignorance crushes culture, and the riff-raff get what they want.
>
> In contrast, many leftist intellectuals denigrate soccer because it castrates the masses and derails their revolutionary ardor. Bread and

> circus, circus without the bread: hypnotized by
> the ball, which exercises a perverse fascination,
> workers' consciousness becomes atrophied and
> they let themselves be led about like sheep by
> their class enemies.[1]

I am most interested in engaging good leftists who do
not take sports or athletes seriously. I think this is valuable
in and of itself for reasons I hope I have articulated over the
past five chapters (!), but also because I think it drags into
the light a critical challenge for the left and radical thought
in general.

One of the great philosophers of sports is the Trinidadian
journalist, cultural critic, Marxist, and political philosopher
CLR James (1901–1989), who was a life-long champion
of cricket, Trotsky, and anti-colonial struggles, maybe
or maybe not in that order. In *Beyond a Boundary*, James
argued that sports (and cricket specifically) could not be
disembedded from larger realities, and that relationships
within cricket did not just mirror larger social relationships,
but constructed them as well. He challenged cricketers to
learn about Marxism, and Marxists to learn to love cricket,
because as Dave Renton wrote in his excellent bio of James:
"If Marxists are unwilling to think the language of sport,
of cricket, and football too, and of all the other games in
which millions spend their leisure, then for whom do we
have any right to speak?"

Bam. Love that, Dave. But why do you think that you,
or Marxists in general, or anyone really should be "speaking *for*" people?[2] Instead can we speak with people, and
more specifically with our neighbors? Can we learn to speak

---

1   Eduardo Galeano, *Soccer in Sun and Shadow*, 33.

2   To be sure I do not want to ascribe this stance to James himself: he
ultimately rejected the notion of the intellectual vanguard and concluded that "every cook can govern."

across difference? I think that's a much more urgent challenge. If we, as radicals or progressives, want to speak with our neighbors, we have to be willing to think and act with respect. And that challenge is issued equally for sports fans and not, athletes and not. It is the specific and compelling challenge of neighborliness: to acknowledge and respect difference where we find it. To be able to speak across difference is to challenge, confront, and admire difference in the embrace of incommensurability.

I think we need to abandon the language of "education," of experts, professionals, vanguards. We need to ask instead: what parts of leftist praxis legitimately support and foster people's capacity toward self-determination? I think that's the heart of it. As Ashanti Alston puts it:

> Either you respect people's capacities to think for themselves, to govern themselves, to creatively devise their own best ways to make decisions, to be accountable, to relate, problem-solve, break-down isolation and commune in a thousand different ways…. Or: you dis-respect them. You dis-respect ALL of us.[3]

We have to be able to trust people's inherent drive and capacity for self-management and self-governance in the workplace, community, neighborhood, household, school, or field. If we don't respect that (subtly or overtly), then we are really calling for renditions of authoritarianism, technocracy, expert-run social milieus, or whatever. Respect has to be a basic political principle.

Obviously, that doesn't mean abdicating our critical faculties. This is not a carte blanche embrace of popular culture per se—that's crazy talk, whether it's Rihanna or Reddit or Rupert Murdoch or Real Madrid. Appreciating

---

3   See http://www.anarchistpanther.net.

difference inheres confrontation, but I do think it's on all of us to treat our friends' and neighbors' passions and interests with real respect and legitimate consideration. And perhaps more than anywhere, people are finding and making meaning in sports, so let's be there. But let's also confront the sporting world's consistent disrespect for those who do not adhere to its often dubious criterions. Sports cannot expect respect without granting it first.

If we take people's passions and creative pursuits seriously (sports and otherwise), then challenging and radicalizing social relationships within sports forces us to recognize that these struggles have a larger social and cultural impact as well. If we want to challenge white supremacy, conversations about black quarterbacks, Cain Velasquez's tattoo, and the Cleveland Indians' logo *really* matter. If we want to talk heteronormativity, Pat Burke matters. And more than just *mattering*, these conversations carry specific and irreplaceable emancipatory possibilities.

Agreed: it is damn hard to appreciate contemporary sports when so much of the sporting world is buried in corporate money. The sheer grossness of it all: the nationalism, the millions and billions of dollars sloshing around, the Olympics, the misogyny, the idiocy … we should never let sports off the hook for any of it. The sporting world is not just a passive recipient of capitalism: sports and athletes are an active and powerful piece of constructing that world. As Eduardo Galeano puts it: "The morals of the market, which in our day are the morals of the world, give a green light to all keys to success, even if they're burglars' tools. Professional soccer has no scruples because it is part of an unscrupulous system of power that buys effectiveness at any price."[4] But what if that were not true? What if sports were a bigger part of constructing a better world? Let me suggest a couple of ideas for starters.

---

4   Eduardo Galeano, *Soccer in Sun and Shadow*, 176.

SPLITTING THE UPRIGHTS

The first place in need of some radical reimagining is the twisted relationship to money, ownership, profit, and control that has consumed the sporting world over the past five decades. A number of intersecting threads have converged to distort the economics of sports beyond anything that's even plausibly alright.

I'm not going to recite absurd stats like the six-billion-plus-over-twenty-five-years regional TV deal the Dodgers just signed with Fox—in part because you know too many of these numbers already, but mostly because by the time you read this book the stats I have on hand right now will be dated, eclipsed in a few months by ever-more absurd contracts and deals. And you know all this: the top echelons of elite athletes make way too much money. Owners make way, way too much money. Pro (and lots of college and amateur) tickets cost way the hell too much. Advertising contracts, TV deals, licensing, apparel, stadiums, boosters, the whole thing is out of any rational control or balance.

All of this is happening in a much-larger, vastly more dangerous economic context, and athletes are well down the list of people who need to have their recompense revisited. Hedge-funders, bankers, investment advisors, advertising execs, CEOs, CFOs …. all these folks (and many more) need their compensation packages radically restructured in a context where worth, merit, and common good have only a passing relationship with paychecks. That said, the economics of sports is not a bad place to consider.

There is obviously a generalized dismay at the economics of sports, but some valuable threads of dissent have emerged in recent years. One of the clearest is around taxpayer-funded stadiums and the multiple practices of siphoning money from public coffers via tax-incentives, subsidies, bonds, relaxations, loans, abatements, and/or sweetheart land deals to help billionaire owners build stadiums. The obvious foolishness of these proposals are nested in larger critiques of public expenditures for private profit, but stadium debates are particularly galling and visible,[5] and voters in numerous cities have resisted (but almost always failed) to keep common money from enriching wealthy owners.

The long-standing claim in favor of stadiums is that they add considerably to the local economy via job creation and local cash injections, but those arguments have been systematically undermined and it has become very clear that stadiums are not a source of local economic growth and employment. Assessing the last NHL hockey lockout, Don Cayo, writing here in Vancouver, found that the stoppage was actually beneficial for the local economy,[6] a phenomenon that has proven true in Canada and the U.S., through a variety of pro sports strikes and lockouts:

> Thorough analyses have shown to be the case time after time—professional sports franchises tend not to boost a local or regional economy, but rather to drag it down a bit....

The empirical evidence supports the heuristic supposition: pro sports teams are big enterprises for sure, but all that money tends to concentrate in the hands of a very few players, owners, and executives. There are some spin-off

---

5 See for good analyses: Dave Zirin, *Bad Sports: How Owners are Ruining the Sports We Love* (2010); Kevin J. Delaney and Rick Eckstein, *Public Dollars, Private Stadiums: The Battle Over Building Sports Stadiums* (2003); Joanna Cagan and Neil deMause, *Field of Schemes: How the Great Stadium Swindle Turns Public Money into Private Profit* (2008); Roger Noll and Andrew Zimbalist (eds.), *Sports, Jobs and Taxes* (2005). *Deadspin* is actually often pretty good on this issue too.

6 Don Cayo, "The NHL lockout was good for Vancouver's Economy," *Vancouver Sun*, January 8, 2013.

economic benefits (bars, restaurants nearby), but essentially, the structure of pro sports and their stadiums tend to concentrate and stagnate wealth. When those sports are in hiatus, people do not just stop spending their entertainment money, it gets spent instead on other things. And those other things tend to disperse the money throughout the city and region better and more equitably. When you put $20 in the pocket of a waitress, for example, the likelihood is that it will get recycled in the community pretty quickly. That same $20 in the pocket of a rich owner will likely end up in an account, holdings, or investments somewhere else.

Aside from the ethical and distributive issues of pro sports economic logic, and the endemic spending of public funds for private profit, there is a simple argument to make in favor of keeping local money circulating locally. And the vast bulk of evidence, even using very conventional analyses, argues against pro sports facilities. The oft-invoked fall-back claim, then, is that governments should subsidize stadiums because the teams carry iconic cultural weight and inculcate civic pride. From an equity point of view, this is problematic and one would be right to ask "what kinds of culture" and "whose pride," but I actually agree to a certain extent with this argument.

I think of Seattle, where the loathsome Clay Bennett moved the once-mighty SuperSonics to Oklahoma City after local and state governments declined to fund a new stadium for the team. That's the team of my youth! Downtown Freddie Brown! Slick Watts! Gus Williams! Dennis Johnson! Jack Sikma! Lonnie Shelton! Paul Silas! Marvin Webster! And of my young adulthood! Shawn Kemp! Gary Payton! Detlef Schrempf! Nate McMillan! That team just cannot be in OKC, especially not with Serge Ibaka, Kevin Durant, and Russell Westbrook. That sweet-ass team should be in Seattle.

I think it is fair to say that Seattle suffered a significant loss when the Sonics left. So did Cleveland with the

Browns, Montreal with the Expos, Winnipeg with the Jets, Buffalo with the Braves, and so many others. It sucks to lose your team, especially if you have invested years, and sometimes decades of care and love. Sure you can cheer for the OKC Thunder (and I do, rather privately), but it sucks. So if a team is a genuine civic resource, a source of pride and identity—then why should those cities and municipalities not own them?

I think that professional sports teams are a public good, and therefore should be publicly accountable and publicly controlled. I'm interested in undermining the logic of profit in every sphere of our lives, but especially the most fundamental, common spheres. At their best, sports teams are community celebrations, expressions of common identity and pride. See for example the incredible confluence of Catalonian culture, language, and independence that adheres around FC Barcelona, a phenomenon repeated (in various, typically less vibrant, renditions) in cities and towns across the globe. So why shouldn't sports teams be commonly owned by the people of their home cities?

There are many examples, the best being the Green Bay Packers, perhaps the most storied and successful franchise in the NFL, with perhaps the most devoted/crazed cheesehead fan base. The Pack represents the smallest city in the league and is the only community-owned pro sports franchise in North America. The team is a non-profit corporation that issues shares in the team, but no dividends are paid, the shares cannot appreciate in value, and while shareholders have voting rights, their shares do not confer any season ticket privileges. No individual can accrue more than 200 shares, so they have a little more than 112,000 shareholders who elect a Board of Directors, which makes it functionally impossible for the team to be moved from Wisconsin, and the financial beneficiary from the team's success is the Green Bay Packers Foundation, which donates to a variety of local charities.

It can be done, and done beautifully. With all the possible creative configurations of ownership that might be devised, is private oligarchical ownership the only one we can come up with in North America? I'll submit to you that we can do better, and if we start thinking of sports and high-performance teams as a common good, repercussive dominoes start to fall. As Julian Ammirante and Tyler Shipley write in *Left Hook Journal*:

> A more radical proposition would be to remove profit from sport altogether. Since sport is in many ways a fundamental part of culture, and communities contribute excessively to the development of the athletes and facilities that pro-leagues exploit, sport should be the property of the community. Organizations structured along non-profit and revenue sharing lines would go a long way to repatriate and reinvigorate sports at all levels and among and across genders. Government policies of building and creating public sporting facilities around the country would revive physical education and personal well-being. Such a scheme would demand a serious evaluation of capitalist ideology, not only in relation to sport, but in relation to economic and political power.[7]

Sports, in fact, are ideally suited to an anti-capitalist thrust. If sports, professional and otherwise, can be infused with a healthier economic logic, then our social and cultural perceptions and expectations of athletes and athletics (at every level) can follow suit.

---

7   Julian Ammirante and Tyler Shipley, "Another NHL Lockout: An Alternative View," *Left Hook Journal*, Sept. 20, 2012.

And, the same is true of our expectations for athletic events. Like, say the freaking Olympics: *the* singular global spectacle, the most effective mega-event for driving neo-liberal transformation, a fiesta of consumptive nationalism for the global tourist class. Of all the possible sporting targets, the five-ring circus is the most worthy of radical critique and transformation, but the Olympics are too gross, too corrupt, too perverted for me to take on properly here. There is a significant and powerful existing literature indicting the IOC, the corporatization of the Games, the maiming of host cities, the fraudulent mercenarism[8]—so let me make one small requisition that applies to smaller international competitions equally.

Among the hardest aspects of the Games to choke down for an anarchist and anti-colonialist is the triumphant nationalism, the celebration of the nation-state as the defining identity of humanity, with all its imperialist and hegemonic implications. But what if athletes could compete under another banner? What if the global athletic competitions represented the world more accurately and appropriately, with people able to compete in a self-organizing, self-defining sets of affiliations?

I'm imagining here a radically restructured, democratized, and cosmopolitan athletic organizational landscape where high-performance athletes can compete under the auspices of cities, community groups, non-profit organizations, cultural affiliations, or just as individuals. This would undercut the colonial fiesta of the Olympics, allow athletes to self-identify their own loyalties, and gesture to a world beyond the nation-state. Look, I know this scenario opens up a barrel of other questions around access and equity, in

---

8   See for example: John Bale and Mette Christensen, *Post Olympism?*; Helen Jefferson Lenskyj, *Olympic Industry Resistance: Challenging Olympic Power and Propaganda*; Mark Perryman, *Why the Olympics Aren't Good for Us, and How They Can Be.*

order to keep the whole thing from devolving into a *Blade Runner*-esque nightmare populated by corporate-sponsored athletes. But with a little good thinking, surely we can imagine a time when global competitions can evolve beyond nationalist spectacle. I'm just saying.

Similarly, there is a thread running through this whole book that invokes the transformation of the ideal of competition: reconstituting it as friendship, not domination—a thread that echoes the plausibility of transforming predatory economics. I'm not talking about evoking some "gentlemanly sportsmanship, be-a-good-sport" ethic, nor am I interested in dispensing with competition as a construct (that strikes me a simultaneously naïve and flakey in a way that even I am not down for), but I am interested in rethinking and redefining and competition.

And really, it's just not that big a leap to think of competition as mutual aid. I suspect that's the way most people actually understand competition in real life: otherwise why would we willingly submit ourselves to it? Sure, there are the hoary sports clichés that a-hole coaches and sportscasters recycle about winning being the only thing, sports as war, etc.—but the vast majority of people I know laugh at that shit because it's not really worthy of consideration. Watch the end of most any game—whether it's a professional ball game, a high-level amateur event, or a friendly at the park—and what happens? Players laugh and talk, inevitably hug and touch each other, joke about successes and failures, go shower, and then head out and drink together.

There is a critical disconnect here between the conceptualization and prefiguration of sports as an antagonist enterprise riddled through with colonial and masculinist narratives that we can reject, in part, if we reject easy definitions of sports. Part of this grates against my sensibilities. My first impulse is be strict: sports require a very discrete set of skills and acts that include speed, strength, quickness, balance, flexibility, and coordination in multiple combinations. Take that one route and hell no, golf isn't a sport. Neither is poker, rummy, tiddlywinks, video games, or anything else you can do sitting down, including driving. Those might be standardized competitions that require physical effort—but vernacularly speaking, forget it. Those are games. Sport = hockey, basketball, soccer, football, tennis, fighting, athletics, swimming, variations on those themes and not a lot else.

But that argument runs into trouble before it gets much out of the gate and is frankly kind of stupid. By that definition how about *Dancing With the Stars*? That's a physically demanding, highly competitive activity that uses multiple combinations of physical skills. So is that a sport or art? How different is that than, say, Olympic-style rhythmic gymnastics, synchronized swimming, or ice-dancing? Even though it's not in the Olympics, the IOC recognizes ballroom dancing as a legit sport. So, by that standard, can most any physical activity be a sport if it is standardized competitively? Rock climbing? Gardening? Bathroom cleaning?

A better route, I'd submit, is to blow that conversation up. Trying to isolate what *is* a sport and what isn't essentially wastes our time:[9] a) there is no difference, those descriptions are entirely socially/culturally constructed, and b) who really gives a shit? I kind of like Louis Menand's attempt to define Olympic sport as ritual. "Games, in my house, were O.K., because games are fun. Sports are games taken much too seriously. Organized sports are an attempt, through regimentation (uniforms and trophies) and rhetoric (rah-rah boosterism and coach talk), to give an inherently pointless activity some kind of point, to inject a purpose into play."[10] Without going all existential about what exactly constitutes "pointless activity" in a vast, meaningless universe, I'd

---

9 Unless you're trying to tweak a golfer, which is not the worst enterprise in the world.

10 Louis Menand, "Glory Days," *The New Yorker*, August 6th, 2012.

respectfully suggest the exact opposite from Louis's claim: really, we should take sports, and games for that matter, way more seriously.

Why not bring sports into a larger constellation of "creative activity"? Instead of constantly categorizing, anatomizing, and gridding as a proto-modernist/positivist exercise that delineates and walls off "sport" from "art" from "game" from "pastime" and on and on into technocratic fantasy, sports should be considered as a form of creative expression like painting, woodwork, music, dance, macramé, rock-wall building, gardening, or any other creative pursuit. It gives us a palette to express ourselves and the chance to appreciate the creative geniuses of others, however they might be expressed.

Indeed, it is creativity that makes and remakes the worlds around us, and one of its bests is the performance of pleasure … or play. I am tempted to try and describe sports as playful collisions with each other and the natural world, and that's not half bad, but I'm not sure that effort escapes the gravitational pull of taxonomy. I want a sporting world that is *always* about joy and playfulness, a creative materiality that, in remaking the word around us, *insists* on pleasure and fun. A reporter once asked the German theologian Dorothee Solle: "How would you explain to a child what happiness is?" "I wouldn't explain it," she answered. "I'd toss him a ball and let him a play."[11]

The playfulness that sports continues to claim, the sheer enjoyment of watching and participating, can be totally undermined by competition. We're all painfully familiar with how the imposition of manipulative competition can ruin our games, turning them bitter and mean, but when reconceptualized as mutual aid, competition injects another layer into our games, far beyond the simple act of keeping score. Competition should have nothing to do with domination. Instead, it can and should push the boundaries

---

11 Galeano, *Soccer in Sun and Shadow*, p. 208.

between singularity and plurality, making permeable the thresholds between discrete bodies, and concretizing solidarity. Understanding competition as mutual aid is so common—athletes of every skill level know the feeling, an intimacy that has nothing to do with the score, but everything to do with commonality ... or friendship.

That possibility of friendship can scarcely be disregarded. As Ivan Illich put it: "I do not believe that friendship today can flower out—can come out—of political life. I do believe that if there is something like a political life to be—to remain for us, in this world of technology—then it begins with friendship ... society will only be as good as the political result of these friendships."[12] And so I return, and end, with my original argument: that the sporting world offers a sweet, powerful, and perhaps irreplaceable avenue for rethinking and remaking this world in which we live.

To be sure, the sporting world has consistently and insistently made the "political result of friendships" repressive, oppressive, and exclusionary. And non-sports fans have justifiably responded in kind. But that is not our fate, and sports are just too important to condescend to.

I started the book asking you to care about sports, whether or not you pay any attention to them or have much interest. I asked you to think about the sporting world as a legitimate site for struggle and politics, for undermining privilege and building solidarity, as a site worthy of respect. The book tries to make a case for why sports matter, or maybe better put, why you should *care* about them. In 1975, Roger Angell wrote something about caring that I think about often.

It is foolish and childish, on the face of it, to affiliate ourselves with anything so insignificant

---

12 Ivan Illich interview with Jerry Brown, *We the People*, KPFA - March 22, 1996.

and patently contrived and commercially exploitative as a professional sports team, and the amused superiority and icy scorn that the non-fan directs at the sports nut (I know this look—I know it by heart) is understandable and almost unanswerable. Almost. What is left out of this calculation, it seems to me, is the business of caring—caring deeply and passionately, really caring—which is a capacity or an emotion that has almost gone out of our lives. And so it seems possible that we have come to a time when it no longer matters so much what the caring is about, how frail or foolish is the object of that concern, as long as the feeling itself can be saved. Naiveté—the infantile and ignoble joy that sends a grown man or woman to dancing and shouting with joy in the middle of the night over the haphazardous flight of a distant ball—seems a small price to pay for such a gift.[13]

I submit to you that this "business of caring" is our best line of defense against neoliberalism. It provides the lived possibility of resistance. In fact, I'll even suggest that caring is a requisite: the quality of our care determines the quality of our resistance. If we can simultaneously reconfigure and encounter sports as worthy of care, then our playful and material collisions can become a pivot point for friendships built on solidarity and difference. And then, perhaps, from there, we can find the right material to remake society.

---

13 Roger Angell, "Agincourt and After," *The New Yorker*, Nov. 17th, 1975: p. 164.

About the author

Matt Hern is a former sportswriter and radical urbanist who lives and works in East Vancouver with his partner and daughters, where he co-founded the Purple Thistle Centre and Car-Free Vancouver Day. His books and articles have been published on all six continents, translated into ten languages and he continues to lecture globally. He holds a PhD in Urban Studies, and teaches at University of British Columbia and Simon Fraser University. He currently devotes his time to directing the Groundswell project in Vancouver. He is the author and editor of numerous works, including *Common Ground in a Liquid City*, *Everywhere All the Time*, and *Stay Solid! A Radical Handbook for Youth*, all published by AK Press.

About AK Press

AK Press is one of the world's largest and most productive anarchist publishing houses. We're entirely worker-run and democratically managed. We operate without a corporate structure—no boss, no managers, no bullshit. We publish close to twenty books every year, and distribute thousands of other titles published by other like-minded independent presses from around the globe.

The Friends of AK program is a way that you can directly contribute to the continued existence of AK Press, and ensure that we're able to keep publishing great books just like this one! Friends pay $25 a month directly into our publishing account ($30 for Canada, $35 for international), and receive a copy of every book AK Press publishes for the duration of their membership! Friends also receive a discount on anything they order from our website or buy at a table: 50% on AK titles, and 20% on everything else. We've also added a new Friends of AK ebook program: $15 a month gets you an electronic copy of every book we publish for the duration of your membership. Combine it with a print subscription, too!

There's great stuff in the works—so sign up now to become a Friend of AK Press, and let the presses roll!

Email friendsofak@akpress.org for more info, or visit the Friends of AK Press website:
www.akpress.org/programs/friendsofak